CHANAKYA'S
100
BEST SUTRAS

CHANAKYA'S 100 BEST SUTRAS

RADHAKRISHNAN PILLAI

JAICO PUBLISHING HOUSE

Ahmedabad Bangalore Chennai
Delhi Hyderabad Kolkata Mumbai

Published by Jaico Publishing House
A-2 Jash Chambers, 7-A Sir Phirozshah Mehta Road
Fort, Mumbai - 400 001
jaicopub@jaicobooks.com
www.jaicobooks.com

CHANAKYA'S 100 BEST SUTRAS
ISBN 978-93-93559-98-2

First Jaico Impression: 2023

Page design and layout: R. Ajith Kumar, Delhi

Printed by
Thomson Press India Limited, New Delhi

CONTENTS

Managing People

Building Relationships

Career Growth

Managing Wealth

Due Diligence

Lifelong Lessons

INTRODUCTION

Consider a mother with many children. Ask her, "Who is your favourite child among all?" Now, you have put the mother in a complete dilemma. She loves all her children equally, and choosing one over the other is not an easy task. In fact, it's emotionally torturous.

I experienced the same feeling while starting to write this book. When the Jaico team asked me to select the 100 finest sutras of Chanakya, it was a mental dilemma for me. Although I am not the creator of any of these sutras — these were originally written by Chanakya, or Kautilya, 2,400 years ago — the predicament was equally intense.

For nearly 25 years, I have been studying, teaching, and writing on Chanakya's teachings. I have come to realise that all his sutras are equally powerful and can transform one forever.

I had the good fortune of studying all the 6,000 sutras of Kautilya's Arthashastra in their original Sanskrit, under the guidance of Dr. Gangadharan Nair from Chinmaya Mission, and later, during my Ph.D, under the mentorship and supervision of Dr. Shubhada Joshi at the University of Mumbai. These great teachers opened up new dimensions of understanding these 6,000 sutras from a modern-day perspective.

So, while I was struggling to select just 100, I prayed to God and my teachers to guide me. Then, as I got onto the task, I remembered these messages from them:

Dr. Gangadharan Nair had said, "There is a Chanakya

hidden inside each one of us. We just need to invoke him and bring out the best in us."

Dr. Shubhada Joshi had guided me, "These ideas of Chanakya are not just imaginations. They are time tested principles and can be applied to our generation to find greater success than in the past."

I have found these statements to be true. Although we (me as an author and Jaico as a publisher) have selected the 100 best sutras from 6,000 sutras for this book, I assure you that the remaining 5,900 sutras are just as powerful. I hope this book will inspire you to read Kautilya's Arthashastra in full someday, guided by great and noble teachers as I was.

Each of these sutras is explained in a simple manner and the methods are easy to apply. Anyone and everyone can understand and follow them in their daily life.

The ocean is large, infinite, and unlimited. So too is the knowledge and wisdom of Chanakya. If you want to understand the ocean, start from the shore nearest you. Similarly, you can start with these 100 sutras to understand Chanakya's wisdom and then continue exploring his other ideas not included in this book.

Read these sutras, reflect upon them, understand their depth, and apply them to your personal and professional life. Then, share your success with others just like you.

While going through these great ideas, remember the goal:

"To bring out the Chanakya in you and to help others to bring out the Chanakya in them."

After all, teaching someone else is one of the best ways of learning.

Dr. Radhakrishnan Pillai

LEADERSHIP

WHY YOU SHOULD READ THE ARTHASHASTRA

"This science [of Arthashastra] brings into being
and preserves spiritual good, material well-being,
and pleasures and destroys spiritual evil, material loss,
and hatred." (15.1.72)

As we start studying the Arthashastra, one may wonder why undertake this exercise at all. Chanakya himself answers this basic yet important question. He says it brings both spiritual and material well-being, help us destroy spiritually evil things, and avoid material or financial loss. And also it helps us prevent hatred towards others and ourselves.

Let us understand the same in detail.

1. Brings and Preserves Spiritual Good

Without a solid spiritual foundation, you cannot become successful in life. Even if you do, your success may not last long. The shaky foundations will eventually cause all you have built to crumble. To avoid this, the Arthashastra helps readers build and preserve what is spiritually good for lasting success.

2. Material Well-Being and Pleasures

What use is it if one is spiritually accomplished but materially poor? In fact, many wrongly believe that this is a common occurrence. But Chanakya breaks this myth. He promises that studying the Arthashastra will also lead to material prosperity. And when we gain wealth this way, we will be able to enjoy all the pleasures of life—ethically.

3. Destroys Spiritual Evil, Material Loss, and Hatred

The Arthashastra also causes destruction. But this is the positive destruction of all that is not spiritually good (like our bad habits and addictions). It destroys the possibility of material loss (like financial or property loss), and we develop a sense of calm and composure. This, in turn, removes hatred towards others.

We find that studying Chanakya's teachings gives us all-round benefits—in this world as well as beyond. This is the beauty of Chanakya's wisdom: He is very practical and gives us a very different approach to life. Those who seek wealth, power, position, etc., will learn how to earn it on the foundation of ethics and values. Those who already have spiritual values will get all the material benefits.

CHANAKYA'S THREE ASPECTS OF SUCCESS

2

"Success is threefold: That attainable by the power of
counsel is success by counsel, that attainable by the
power of might is success by might, and that attainable by
the power of energy is success by energy." (6.2.34)

Chanakya wants us to be successful, and he gives us various
methods to help us to this end. These methods can be
practiced by anyone at anytime. But what are these three types
of success: by counsel, by power of might, and energy? Let's see.

1. Success by Power of Counsel

An adviser is crucial in every undertaking, and each person needs
one. Many already tend to seek the advice of an expert before
starting any work. But, at the same time, be careful of the person
whom you are taking advice from. An adviser can make you or
break you. But once you find the right adviser, who truly cares
for your well-being, success is guaranteed. This is the success we
get through the power of good counsel.

Shri Krishna is the best example of a good adviser. He guided the Pandavas on the battlefield. Even when things looked bleak, he stood by them, saving them from the Kauravas through his counsel. As a result, the Pandavas, with little military power and vastly outnumbered, won the war.

2. Success by Power of Might

Muscle power and strength can also influence outcomes. Might also means the benefits one gets from their power of position. A mighty person can make many quick decisions based on his authority. Through his execution capacity, the person can succeed.

If one is not mighty, one can also gain might by association with another powerful person. Over time, you may pick up their traits, and even mimic their power and success. Going back to the example of Shri Krishna, Arjuna chose to have Krishna on his side, while Duryodhana chose the Yadava army in the battle of Kurukshetra. Though outmatched and outnumbered, Arjuna still emerged victorious by this association.

3. Success by Energy

The power of sheer will, drive and passion—which is constantly energising one—can't be understated in the quest for success either.

These traits are also contagious by their very nature. When one is surrounded by an energetic person, even a lazy person will get charged up. All great leaders have this quality, which makes them powerful. They can inspire others with their speeches and oratory skills.

So if you want to be successful, follow either of these three methods. Better still, follow all three methods—success will be guaranteed.

RECOGNISE THE REAL POWER BEHIND THE KINGS

3

"He who sees policies as being interdependent plays as he pleases, with kings tied by the chains of their intellect." (7.18.44)

The leaders are in power and in the power game. But not many people understand real power, even if they command it. There is a general assumption that the person sitting on the chair is the most powerful person—the president, prime minister, chief minister, chairperson, director, etc.

But the reality is different; a few intelligent people, who may not appear to be in power, run the world. They make policies and strategies for others. Such people even tie up the leaders (kings) with their intelligence.

So, who are the people who are more powerful than the kings?

1. Gurus or Teachers

Teachers or gurus play a vital role in the life of a king or leader. Whatever the names you give them, their opinion and inputs matter whenever you are in a moral dilemma. Through their vast exposure and experience, their instruction can highly influence even a powerful person's thinking.

2. Advisors

No influential person will take any decision without the consent of his advisors. These advisors, always present behind the scenes, may hardly be noticed in public. But their word can make or break any leader—it can significantly affect the way a nation or organisation functions. They are the main change agents. So, it's important that one seek advice from experts from various fields for effective decision making.

3. Friends

Then, there is the group of friends. In the Arthashastra, they are called *mitras*. A leader must be very careful when selecting a friend, for there are good and bad people out there.

Broadly, there are two types of friends a leader can have. Those who were his friends before he became a leader and others who became friends after he became a leader. One must carefully scrutinise the second type as they may have vested interests. After all, these people will soon become more powerful than the king, being able to influence his thought.

So always consider this: Who are the people who influence the king's thought process?

THE SPIRITUAL SIDE OF WORKING RIGHT

4

"Carrying out his own duty, the king who protects
the subjects according to law goes to heaven; one who
does not protect or who inflicts unjust punishment, his
condition would be reverse of this." (3.1.41)

The leader of any country or organisation must fulfil many
responsibilities. They have to be aware of all their duties
and work towards the betterment of the society.

Among the most important duties of the leader is to ensure
the security and safety of the citizens, create good economic
conditions, revenue for the government, and recognise and
reward contributors of society. If these duties are fulfilled, the
leader will be praised by his citizens. Also, he experiences
benefits in this world and the other worlds.

So, how does one become an "ideal leader" with spiritual
understanding?

1. Perform Your Duties Properly

Every leader must become a "role model". Lead by example. All eyes in the kingdom are fixed on the leader. So, rather than making empty talk, follow your duties properly. On doing so, you'll find others follow suit. If you fail, the others will do the same. So, understand your duties and deliver the results expected from a leader. The daily duties of a king (leader) is given in book 1, chapter 19 of Kautilya's Arthashastra. They will guide you to understand the rules for the king. Read the chapter and follow the instructions given.

2. Respect the Law

Leaders create laws. However, even though the king is a law unto himself he should never cross the limits and remember that, apart from the human-made laws, there are natural laws. Both must be respected equally. The leader needs to also guide others in following them. When the whole society is in sync with the law (dharma), everyone is happy. A dharmic, or "law abiding", society is what Chanakya and all great thinkers wanted to create.

3. Be Just

Delivering justice is among a leader's foremost responsibilities. If there is a conflict, the subjects will come to the leader seeking a resolution. At such times, integrity can help resolve issues justly and in the right manner. The Arthashastra tells us about the right method of punishing offenders. If too many are punished, it leads to the citizens living in fear. However, if no punishments are given, the king is taken for granted.

The right use of punishment comes from the leader's wisdom. In case the leader does not know what to do, they can seek legal counsel and act accordingly. In today's organisations, legal and human resources departments execute this function.

TO BE OR NOT TO BE, THAT IS THE QUESTION

5

"The affairs of a king [leader] are [of three kinds, viz.]
directly perceived, unperceived, and inferred." (1.9.4)

L ife is all about taking decisions. A delay in making timely
decisions leads to loss of not only time and money, but also
energy.

Therefore, we must be very careful while taking decisions.
The first step to good decision-making is to collect the right
information from the right sources. Once we collect the data,
next is to analyse it. To ensure that the process is effective, he
breaks down the information that needs to be analysed into three
types.

1. Directly Perceived

Heard the adage seeing is believing? Directly perceived
information is the most authentic form of information one can
gather, as one has witnessed it firsthand. There are many leaders
who, solitarily sitting in their offices, eventually lose control over

their people. They rely on second-hand information, relayed by others. While useful, this also presents a risk: their staff can take them for a ride. To avoid this, a leader must always be perceptive of the ground level reality and periodically mingle with the staff and clients. This exposure will help them gather reliable information and act accordingly.

2. Unperceived

As human beings we have limitations. We cannot be in all places at all times. Nonetheless, we may use other sources to gather information. Any information that reaches you in such a manner is unperceived. Technology facilitates this at a blazing pace, helping us gather real-time information from multiple locations simultaneously.

3. Inferred

The ability to see what is not seen by gathering insights and arriving at a conclusion is called inference. It could also mean making projections about the future using information from prior experiences. For example, looking at smoke one can infer that there is a fire. In this case, even though one has not seen the fire directly, smoke is one of the indicators of the fire.

Keen observations and tremendous experience go into making good decisions. A mature person can analyse any given situation within few moments. After all, experience is an insightful teacher and helps them acquire the "knack" of quick decision-making. Such individuals can also offer foresights.

So, whenever you must make a critical decision, consider its type, think critically with an open mind using your insights. Your gut will accordingly direct you to the answer.

THE LEADER HAS TO BE A ROLE MODEL

6

"When all laws are perishing, the king here is the promulgate of laws by virtue of his guarding the right conduct of the world consisting of the four varnas and four asramas." (3.1.38)

In Sanskrit, "law" is called *dharma*, meaning "that which holds". What keeps society from becoming a disorderly mess? Laws. If they were missing, people would be out of control. Our lives would become filled with utter chaos and confusion.

In many cases, these laws are unwritten. However, in organisations and countries, they are documented as principles, rules, regulations, policies, mission statements, constitutions, etc. Chanakya suggests that if these laws have not been set down and formalised yet, the king (leader) should take the lead in doing so.

But, before you do that, one has to ask themselves the following:

1. A Law for What?

Laws must always serve a purpose. Until that is not made clear, we will just be acting mechanically without any clarity of the goal. In some organisations "rule-setting" is merely conducted as a formality. It has no depth or human element. Sometimes, even compliance and governance-related documents are signed without even knowing why they are required and the stipulations inside. As a leader, it is important to have a clear vision about the laws and rules that are getting created.

2. Will it Benefit All?

Kautilya always reminds the king or leader about his fundamental duty: to consider the benefit of all his subjects and act accordingly. When they are making a policy, they must consider the benefit of all and not just their own. The welfare of all is the foundation on which a society, nation, country, or an institute is built. If this is missing, then the subjects will be disappointed and, in the long run, will either replace their leader or search for a new one.

3. Is it Fit for All?

In the quoted verse, Chanakya advises the king should make laws according to the four varnas and asramas. This means that we are considering various aspects of the population or staff— age, talents, and natural qualities—while taking various policy decisions. For example, a poor, starving person stealing bread out of desperation may be let off unpunished. This is because the act or stealing was a matter of survival for him rather than greed.

Such human consideration while making laws is important.

LEADERS UPFRONT HAVE THE EDGE

"If the king is energetic, his subjects will be equally energetic. If he is slack [and lazy in performing his duties] the subjects will also be lazy and thereby eat into his wealth. Besides, a lazy king will easily fall into the hands of the enemies. Hence the king should himself always be energetic." (1.19.1-5)

This is one of Chanakya's most powerful sutras. All those in leadership positions must use this as a guiding light. In fact, I would even request you, the reader, to keep a constant reminder of this—put it up on a wall or even on your mobile screen.

The leader has the most critical role to play in taking the country or the organisation ahead. Being at the helm, they must guide others and help them achieve higher goals, innovate, and set new trends. This is how Chanakya defines the ideal leader. A self-motivated person, it falls upon the leader to raise the enthusiasm of his team members. This is only possible if the leader is energetic. If he is lazy, his team members will also become lazy in their work. Very soon, a sense of complacency will take over.

But can you cultivate energy? There are three levels to consider.

1. Physical Activity

Get up and get going. When the body moves, everything moves. Lethargy is slow poison. Perform exercises, practice yoga, and make sure you push your body so it can grow. Over time, you would be surprised how it affects your mind and makes it active in turn. Remain physically active and you will feel energetic.

2. Mental Fortitude

The mind will play a lot of games and try to control you. However, you must take control. Think of the mind as a monkey; it never likes to sit still. Instead, it keeps jumping from one place to another, from one thought to another. But you must take the wheel and give it direction.

The best way to do this is by practicing meditation. It helps us watch our mind and slowly bring it under our control. Once this mental energy is controlled and channelised in a productive direction, it can create wonders.

3. Intellectual Conviction

Intellectual conviction comes from the study of great literature and various kinds of philosophical and enriching books. Staying in touch with current affairs and developing critical thinking and analytical skills to understand various issues is also vital. If we surround ourselves with intellectual people more geared to thinking this way, we too will grow wiser. This leads to intellectual conviction, and a person who has attained it can energise others with the clarity of their thought and effective communication.

BEING ENERGETIC IS THE KEY TO SUCCESS

"Bravery, resentment, quickness, and dexterity—these are the qualities of energy." (6.1.5)

Chanakya now tells us the different qualities of energy. It does not mean non-stop activity or being loud—both are simply attention-seeking tactics. Here the four qualities are part of the person's personality. Let us look at these in detail.

1. Bravery

Courage in the face of frightening or unpleasant things sets good leaders apart from great ones. A brave person is ready to face life's unpleasant events with a strong heart and tremendous will power to carry on. Such a person is ready to fight and conquer challenges along the journey towards their goal.

2. Resentment

Resentment—anger, hatred, and bitterness—is often considered a negative quality. However, we need to understand this a bit differently. It means being unsatisfied with our present state. In healthy amounts, dissatisfaction can push us towards achieving bigger things in life. We get motivated to do better. A person who is angry with one's own unintelligent thought, hates laziness, and is a bitter towards small achievements, wants to change for better. Such a quality makes one beat lethargy.

3. Quickness

Quickness does not mean being impulsive. It means making sound decisions at short notice. After all, time is an important factor for success.

If you want to learn to be quick, be around people who are not afraid of making mistakes. Not the kind of people who act on foolish impulses and repeat mistakes but and focused people make for better company. Think like a fighter pilot. Learn to act soundly even under pressure, when the stakes are high. Every millisecond counts.

4. Dexterity

Dexterity is the ability to adapt and continue despite challenges. A popular American witticism reads, "When the going gets tough, the tough gets going." We all start on a journey, but not all adapt to the changes, navigating through issues, finding solutions, and overcoming problems. We should always be ready to adapt, though it is not easy.

When you are truly energetic with these qualities, you will be crowned with success in every activity you undertake.

BEING THERE:
AN OPEN-DOOR POLICY

9

"He [leader] should allow unrestricted entrance to those
wishing to see him in connection with their affairs."
(1.19.26)

Among the leader's greatest assets is awareness that they might
receive wrong as well as manipulative information from
various sources. They must scrutinise these sources closely to
avoid misguidance.

Many leaders tend to become overly dependent on their
informers. This can be very dangerous. Dependence breeds
various harmful possibilities. Middle-men can modify reports,
become corrupt, and leak important data. Therefore, Kautilya
advises an open-door policy to the leaders. Intermediaries should
not be able to restrict or control who meets the leader and shares
information with them. This direct communication will help
bridge the gap between the leader and the led.

In many organisations, one has to go through endless barriers
to get to the top. This is sub-optimal. Yes, the person may have

to be checked for security reasons, but access should be given to the last man in the hierarchy to approach the one at the top. This kind of open-door policy has many benefits.

1. Direct Information

Many times, when people come to meet the leader, they can give a lot of direct information about the ground realities. When many are enabled to do so, the leader gains eyes and ears throughout the kingdom—an all-round flow of information from multiples sources. This allows for a 360° view of matters, reducing the possibility of misinformation. They can keep a direct check and feel the pulse of what others are thinking at the grassroots. As a bonus, this also helps identify internal competitors and enemies.

However, most external threats come from people's internal insecurities, felt by our own people. So listen to your people and you will be loved by all.

2. Avoiding External Threats

When the common man is assured that they are heard, they will not want for the help of external agencies. Remember, competitors enemy is always waiting for an opportunity to lure dissatisfied people in your circle and create an internal disturbance. Divide and rule is only one way to snatch power—many more treacherous methods exist.

3. Faster Decisions

Important decisions do not get delayed when problems are fixed as they occur. Timely decisions help avoid confusion and misunderstandings. Speed is of the essence, and an open-door policy helps improve just that.

4. Emotional Bonding

Everyone feels a deep emotional bond with the leader who reassures them of support in their joys and sorrows. When people can share their concerns with the leader, it builds a sense of security and faith.

One of the basic human psychological needs is to have someone who can listen to you. Effective leaders understand this need. So they send a message to others: "I will be there whenever you have a problem."

THE POWER OF COMMUNICATION

10

"Defamation, vilification, and threat constitute
verbal injury." (3.18.1)

A school once surveyed a batch who had graduated 20 years
ago. Surprisingly, the successful ones were not the academic
toppers but those who knew how to work in teams; more
importantly, they had good communication skills.

Chanakya knew the power of communication well. In fact, he
highlighted how it is easy to use words as weapons. Unwise word
choice can lead to defamation, vilification, and even threat. He
went one step further and guided on avoiding such words which
constitute verbal injury.

Every person requires appreciation. If you cannot appreciate
others, you can certainly avoid using the wrong words leading to
the below mentioned three.

1. Defamation

This is used often as a tool by people to get public support.

Anyone who becomes successful is exposed to public insult and defamation. However, they also hold the power to defame others and tend to abuse it. Such acts dent their credibility and impact goodwill. One should avoid defaming anyone unless they have their facts right.

2. Vilification

Painting someone as the villain is common. Remember the rule, "If you want to appreciate someone, do it in public. If you want to tell them about the wrongdoings, do it in private." This way, the person will not feel insulted and will take the message in the right spirit. Speaking person-to-person is the best way to offer feedback to another.

3. Threat

Threats snatch a sense of security from the threatened. Leaders who communicate ineffectively may often find themselves in a situation where their followers are threatened. They must avoid such outcomes. Do not try to infuse fear in a person unless it is absolutely critical. For instance, if someone threatens you, then you should also be strong and respond in kind for your own safety. But, under normal circumstances, do not use threats as a tool. As per Chanakya this is a crime.

The best way to communicate is in a soft, yet firm manner. It is said in the Ramayana that King Rama was an effective communicator. He could communicate in a truthful (*satyam*) and a pleasing (*priyam*) manner.

Develop these qualities of communication to succeed in life.

DO NOT FEAR OR MAKE OTHERS FEARFUL

"He should turn away from frightful words and should not himself use frightful words to another, and should tolerate [such words] addressed to himself being full of forbearance like the earth." (5.4.15)

Leadership is about using your power selflessly in the right manner. Influence is best used to serve others. Do not make your juniors frightened of you. Instead, be patient like mother earth, who endures everything we do to her.

Chanakya gives the same advice to followers (employees). One should turn away from the frightful words of the king (leader)—meaning, in case the leader is unhappy or angry, just be quiet. Those emotions may be temporary and the leader will address your concerns when he cools off.

Let us see how to practise this in our daily lives.

1. Do Not React

Animals live on impulse. Stimuli rule their lives. When they feel hungry, they eat. When they feel frightened, they run. When they are tired, they sleep. Their intellects are limited and not as developed as ours.

So when you are around powerful people, they may react to you negatively. But you should not be provoked. Learn to relax instead. It may so happen that your reaction adds fuel to the fire, escalating matters. Learn to take a deep breath and let your intellect take over your mind.

2. Learn to Respond

If one is not reacting, then what should the person do? They should learn to respond instead. Pause and think through issues. When you don't think, you react. When you think and take measured steps, you respond.

Think through all consequences when you are with the leader, or even when you are a leader yourself. When prompted to make important decisions, take some time if you must. If required, consult experts. This way you will apply your intellect and take the right decisions.

3. Make it a Habit

Habits can be incredibly powerful. However, installing them begins with small, consistent steps. With practice, it becomes ingrained in you to respond and not react. By and by, it will become your nature. So be mindful of your actions.

Some say that getting angry is in their nature. But, you can change your nature by practising the right habits. Start one day at a time. Even if, initially, you can only control your anger in a few instances, you make a good start. As you train your mind, you'll feel calmer in more stressful situations. Then, over days of practice, you will be a natural at keeping calm and being composed.

NEVER FORCE ANYONE TO ACCEPT YOUR VIEWS

"Touching, menacing and striking constitute
physical injury." (3.19.1)

There are many who force their views on others. In their
heads, it either their way or the highway. Such arrogance
and rigidity—almost dictatorial in nature—make them unideal
leaders.

They will not think twice before putting others in harm's way.
Physical injury is often the most common route taken. They
misuse their powers and even kill others—far from the type of
leaders that Chanakya wanted to create. He wanted leaders who
will take care of their people and lead them by example.

In the above sutra, Chanakya describes the three types of
physical injuries one should avoid inflicting when dealing with
others.

1. Touching

There are different types of physical contact. In everyday life,
when you touch people physically, it arouses different emotions.

This may be good feelings like love, sympathy, and kindness—positive in nature, making one feel cared, loved, and needed. In fact, research shows that such positive touching can boost our immunity, lower blood pressure, and relax us.

But, touch that causes physical injury disturbs a person, both physically and mentally. Therefore, it is ill-advised to touch anyone with hatred or negative emotion directed at them. Chanakya disallows it under all circumstances.

2. Menacing

People in power weild symbols of their authority. These also come in the form of rod, guns, or swords. Sometimes, those who weild them, forget that authority is not to be used for display of power on those less powerful than you. It should be used for protection and safety of others. Therefore, Chanakya prohibits threatening someone, even if one doesn't intend to act on it.

3. Striking

Power, taken to its extreme, is manifested through striking—causing tangible physical harm. This too is ill-advised according to Chanakya. Even the police department cannot exercise violence—use guns and weapons—at their discretion. They must wait for orders, and if they do use it, an explanation has to be presented in the report. At one end, if it is misused, even the policemen can be punished. At the other end, if they kill the enemy with the same weapon for the protection of others, they are rewarded.

Chanakya's clear message is this: Never use your power to harm anyone physically or to cause physical injury.

GAME THEORY: THE ART OF TACKLING YOUR COMPETITOR

"If near him [enemy], he should strike
in his weak point." (7.2.12)

Chanakya is known for his strategic thinking. Here is a very important point he discusses about warfare, which can be used in various aspects of life.

An enemy is someone whom we want to defeat. And Chanakya teaches us the art of winning. Every winner waits for the opportunity to strike the enemy. A move that guarantees the final win. "Strike the enemy at their weakest," he says. The enemy may have a lot of strengths, but knowing their weakness is the key to victory.

Here's how you can put this sutra into practice:

1. Observe and Study the Enemy

The more you examine an enemy, the better you get to know them. Be mindful that every enemy is different, and remain vigilant. Observe their moves. Study their nature and behaviour. Understand their strengths and weakness. Never take them for granted. Try and understand their purpose and goals. When you finally figure out their modus operandi, their operating patterns, the next course of action will become clear to you.

2. Be Cautious

The enemy may look harmless, but do not take them at face value. Many who look soft and calm from the outside are dangerous from the inside. They may even be scheming against you.

Therefore, be on the guard. This does not mean you should be frightened of the enemy. Just be fully prepared for the conflict that could break out at any moment.

3. Strike When the Opportunity Comes

When you get the right opportunity, strike!

This is the perfect move. The one stroke to victory. After a long period of watching and preparing for the eventuality, you finally have the window to act—a shot at success.

Recall how the lion goes for its prey. In a herd of deer, it keenly observes the weakest one. Among many options, he chooses the "one" that he wants to attack and slowly starts to make his move, inching closer to it. And, at the right time, he strikes and catches it in one go.

Among many, choose one weakness. And with careful planning, execute your move perfectly.

TIPS FOR STAYING AT THE TOP

14

"Control over senses, which is motivated by training
in the sciences, should be secured by giving up *kaam*,
krodha, *lobha*, *mana*, *madh*, and *harsha*." (1.6.1)

Self-discipline is the key ingredient for success in life. If you
can control yourself, you can control the world. On the flip
side, even if the world is under your control and you cannot
moderate your actions, you will lose all your power. Therefore,
while training leaders, Chanakya ensured they developed
Indriya-Jaya, or "a victory over the senses."

1. *Kaam* (Lust) and *Krodha* (Anger)

Lust means a strong desire for something. In a leadership
context, the lust for power and position is most common: a trap
good leaders must avoid.

Anger, on the other hand, is among the most common
negative qualities we possess. Not controlled, it leads to total
destruction. But the good news is that, with steady practice, one
can overcome this destructive emotion.

2. *Lobha* (Greed) and *Mana* (Pride)

"The world has enough for everyone's needs but not everyone's greed," said Gandhiji. A greedy person may seem active and dynamic, but their energy has a negative, selfish quality. Service is not the top thing on their mind. Chanakya strove to create leaders who would inspire others and not greed for power.

Also, there is a big difference between a person with self-respect and pride and one with self-respect and dignity. Pride instils a feeling of superiority, which in turn leads to arrogance. However, feeling inferior to others—the other extreme—drains your confidence. Therefore, one should pair self-respect with dignity. Chanakya would train every leader to hold their heads high and march towards success. Still, humility and gentleness take on equal importance. Should you let your pride swell, fall is guaranteed.

3. *Madh* (Arrogance) and *Harsha* (Over-Excitement)

Arrogant leaders think of themselves as all-powerful and faultless. They do not like getting feedback or critical input from others, ignoring them in favour of his own plans. Chanakya's ideal leader, however, listens to the common man and takes decisions for their well-being.

Being equanimous is essential for a leader. But over-excitement and extreme moods can be dangerous. Therefore, it is said that leaders should not be impulsive but rational and even-minded in all situations.

DON'T IGNORE POLITICS OR EVEN POLITICIANS

15

"A king who has not learnt the teaching of the science of politics is unfit to listen to counsel." (1.15.61)

Remember how Chanakya exacted his revenge on King Dhanananda? After the king disrespected him, Chanakya took Chandragupta under his wing. Only after years of vigorous training did the young boy blossom into a powerful king.

Training is key for every king or leader. People often become leaders without proper training, only to realise that they would have performed better if they had trained earlier. Chanakya believed that we should make one a leader only after training, especially in politics and dealing with others. After all, only training in the science of politics makes one fit to listen to counsel. This will also make the individual mentally, intellectually, morally, and spiritually ready to take the position. Otherwise, even if there is position and power on your side, it is only a matter of time before you will be ousted.

1. The "Science" of Politics

Politics must be approached scientifically. It is a logical and systematic process of governance. Usually, the first thing that comes to mind when we think of politics is corrupt politicians. But does not everyone aspire to have productive leaders and politicians who can help society progress?

Unfortunately, not many leaders understand the ethics and philosophy related to politics. They only look at the legal aspects. After all, who is better respected: the wise, sensible politician or a power-hungry one who plays on legal loopholes to gain power?

Chanakya, therefore, first teaches the philosophy of leadership (*aanvikshiki*) along with science of politics (*raja vidya*)

2. Listening

Listening—not hearing—is the next important skill to learn. When you listen, you engage with what you hear: thinking, analysing, and empathising. You feel their sentiments. Thoughtful listening, as a result, makes one an effective communicator.

Develop the listening quality. An easy way to practice this is by listening to elders and children. Both are in different stages of their lives and offer differing perspectives.

3. Taking Counsel

Once you have studied the science of politics and your listening honed your skills, you are ready to take counsel. Traditionally, counsel is offered by elders and experts. But are you prepared to take it? You may be surrounded by experts, but very few takers for their experience and wisdom exist.

Here, Chanakya places special importance on elders. He considers it a loss to any society when elders' opinions are neglected. Their understanding of various dimensions of life can become a guiding map for us all.

WHAT A LEADER SHOULD NOT DO

"Reasons for dissatisfaction of subjects: Discarding the good and favouring the wicked."(7.5.19-26)

Subjects may grow unhappy with the king for various reasons. Chanakya points out two major reasons for this unhappiness—discarding the good and favouring the wicked. If a king or leader does not support the good but instead favours the wicked, he will be ousted quickly. Chanakya clearly says that a leader should avoid this trap for his subjects' happiness. So, how does the leader avoid them? The Arthashastra offers insights:

1. Be Aware of Ground Realities

There are a variety of people around us, from saints to criminals. Since we cannot avoid either, we should have a full grip on every occurrence. This requires immense effort and planning, along with surveillance systems.

Chanakya, for example, had created a well-oiled information network that gave him insights into activities outside and inside the palace. These informers would meet the king daily, and he would take necessary actions. The leader would also, from time to time, go to the villages and cities to inspect various activities.

This applies in modern-day offices as well. The advice is simple: Don't confine yourself to your cubicle. Go out and engage.

2. Honour the Good

When he finds good people who are productive and contribute to the overall well-being, the leader should honour them publicly. Modern research even indicates rewards and recognition boosts work motivation and job satisfaction. This could be in the form of rewards or gestures of acknowledgement. This will inspire them to continue doing good work. Moreover, it cements a positive impression of the leader in their minds. Countries and organisations across the globe confer awards for this reason. These gems shine in front of others and create more gems.

3. Punish the Wicked

Anti-social elements, on the other hand, must be punished. In society, they come in the form of robbers, murderers, and scammers—criminals in general. We can try to reform them. However, doing so is not possible in all cases. Then, punishment is necessary. Right punishment, in the right degree for the right person, brings the leader honour and respect. Moreover, the sight of punishment can deter future offenders as well.

MANAGING
PEOPLE

HOW TO WORK WITH A POWERFUL PERSON

"Fire, when it reaches another, may burn a part of the body or the whole, but a king might kill one along with sons and wife, or might cause one to prosper." (5.4.17)

Leaders have the power to both create and destroy. Therefore, we must be cautious while dealing with powerful people. In this sutra, Chanakya explains the concept with the example of fire. It helps us with an array of things. However, it can also severely harm us and even prove fatal.

So, how do we benefit from the leader instead of being destroyed?

1. Serve the Leader

Do not be a threat if you are part of the leader's team. Instead, be of service to him. The moment you become a threat, they will act to defend their position and destroy you in the process. But, with the right attitude, you gain the leader's trust.

Those who gain the leader's trust will be given more opportunities. They and their family will be taken care of.

2. Have a Long-Term Approach

Do not change your organisation or leader for trivial and petty reasons. Those who change jobs regularly are often mistrusted.

Therefore, be committed for the long term. The benefits will be much more significant. Imagine a leader who has two team members: one has only recently joined, whereas the other has been with them for a long time. Naturally, the one who has shown long-term commitment will be favoured over the other.

3. You Will Get More Than You Desire

Under the care and concern of the leader, you may get several benefits—often more than what you desire or deserve. There have been many cases where servants of kings were granted kingdoms and became kings themselves. Similarly, an organisation favours a loyal employee for promotions and awards. Clearly, there are many benefits to this model, and it is only natural: serve, and you shall receive—often much more than expected.

ALL FOR ONE AND ONE FOR ALL

18

"Rulership can be successfully carried out [only] with
the help of associates. One wheel alone does not turn.
Therefore, he should appoint ministers and listen to
their opinion." (1.7.9)

L eadership is difficult. It may look glamorous from the
outside, but it is really a stressful position with many
responsibilities. Everyone is dependent on the leader's decisions.
As a result, if the leader makes a mistake, everyone suffers.

Chanakya reveals how to make the role easier. Mentor others
to support you in your role. As in a vehicle, one wheel alone
makes for a misbalanced mess. Similarly, a leader cannot lead
alone. Here is what Chanakya recommends:

1. Appoint the Right Ministers

Ministers, or managers under the leader, are key resources.
They are the core team. Without them, the leader cannot move

ahead and take the right decisions. Therefore, they must master appointing the right person for the job.

Book one of the Arthashastra details the appointment of such people. They are selected only after a round of tests that establish trustworthiness. Once a part of the core team of the leader, they are expected to perform to their best ability.

2. Listen to Their Opinion

The ministers are intellectuals and thinkers themselves. So respect them—listen to them. If you simply give them orders, you breed discontent. The best way to show this respect is by consulting them regularly.

The ministers can also contribute to debates and discussions, especially when the leader is at crossroads. If the minister does not have a counter-view, he is probably not a good thinker who can offer new perspectives and a different point of view. This can be a great value addition to the decision-making process.

3. Together We Win

The overall objective of the king-minister or leader-deputy relationship is the overall benefit of the nation or organisation. When they think, plan, and execute projects together, they also win together.

They inspire each other to reach common goals, leading to the overall happiness of the citizens.

DELEGATION OF TASKS

19

"Because of the simultaneity of undertakings, their manifoldness and their having to be carried out in many different places, he [leader] should cause them to be carried by ministers, unperceived [by him], so that there is no loss of place and time." (1.9.8)

Imagine yourself as a country's president or prime minister. You bear responsibility for everything in the country, from national security to providing sources of income for the people, promoting cultural activities, and acknowledging and rewarding exceptional contributors.

But one person alone cannot handle everything. So there must be a system; key individuals should be appointed for every role, ensuring everything functions efficiently.

Chanakya is giving us direction on how to take care of multitasking as a leader.

1. Work Occurs Simultaneously at Different Places

The world is a dynamic place. It is continuously in flux, and many events transpire concurrently. And the management machinery should take care of various activities at different places by different departments.

Usually, the general public interacts with government offices and political leaders. But numerous departments—the municipality, police, and army—work round the clock to maintain smooth functioning.

2. Unperceived [By Him]

Efficient systems never require micromanagement. To ensure this, the right people should be performing tasks they are most competent at. However, they must be trained upon induction and later through continuous learning programs as they settle into their roles. Doing so also familiarises them the organisation's vision, making them independent decision-makers. The result? The organisation can operate without the leader's interference in daily matters, allowing them to focus on the bigger picture.

3. No Loss of Time

If such a system and the right people exist, there is no loss of time—the process is quick and effective. After all, justice delayed is justice denied. In the same vein, if work is not completed promptly, it piles up and becomes challenging to manage.

Chanakya envisions a leader's office to be efficient, productive, and secure. Of course, this is only achievable when administrative machinery has perfect systems and processes. But such systems can only materialise when the leader and the right ministers efficiently work toward one common goal. This vision keeps the nation (or an organisation) progressive and prosperous.

THE ART OF BRAIN-STORMING A PROBLEM

20

"In an urgent matter, he should call together the councillors as well as the council of ministers and ask them. What the majority among them declare or what is conducive to the success of the work, that he [leader] should do." (1.15.58-59)

There are always urgent matters requiring urgent decisions. Unfortunately, most time-sensitive issues are resolved impulsively. In such cases, it is only a matter of time before the choices lead to disaster.

Chanakya offers a solution. If one follows this process as given in the above sutra, proper and productive decisions will be taken. This will lead to everyone's overall benefit.

1. Call Your Team Together

A leader must always have a core team or a group of advisors who are knowledgeable and experienced. They are friends, philosophers, and guides; they can offer rich insights and perspectives in the face of challenges.

Best of all, they will have different opinions, stimulating discussions and revealing new possibilities. This also helps you to be more confident. However, the final execution must be done by ministers and their teams.

2. Discuss with Them

You may not have enough time at your disposal. It is like an enemy who has already arrived at your borders, ready to attack. Chanakya, however, advises that one should not rush to decisions. Instead, take some time to discuss and gather opinions and arrive at your own analysis.

It is like sharpening a blunt knife before you start cutting. This preparedness makes the task easier in the long term. Never be impulsive; be a constant learner, sharpening your intellect through advisors and team members.

3. Act

Now that the decision is taken, act quickly. The urgent matter, discussed and decided, should be executed well. Remember, no decision is great by itself—it must be complemented by action and results.

TAKE CARE OF ALL COMPONENTS TO ENSURE GROWTH

21

"There is no country without people, and no kingdom without the country." (18.4.5)

Here, "country" stands for the rural villages or the countryside. Gandhiji, the father of our nation, said, "India lives in its villages." He understood the real heart of India is in its rural areas, and that made him a mass leader because he could connect to the common person in a more profound manner.

Even though we are a generation that aspires to migrate to cities and later to foreign countries, we should not overlook on the value our villages add. Those who understand this will rule the world.

Chanakya is guiding us to the eternal fact that people make a village, and villages make a kingdom. Let us understand this in detail.

1. People

Human beings are social creatures—we are an interdependent species that require each other for our basic survival. We start life as dependent individuals and later aspire to independence. However, maturity and wisdom tell us that we are an *interdependent* species. Isolation takes a toll on our mental health.

Each person may have independent opinions and views, but we exist collectively and collaboratively. Therefore, mutual respect becomes the foundation of every culture and civilisation.

2. Countryside or Villages

The smallest unit of human society is the family. When many families join, they form a village where we grow as one unit. Even in the globalised world, social thinkers aim for the world as one "global village."

It is said, "You require a village to bring up a child." Not just a family but a collective—a village, in this case—to shape the person from birth till death. Chanakya recognises this and appreciates them as the grassroots of society.

3. Kingdom

A king needs to understand his kingdom and the people living there. Such a leader can connect with the furthest man in the most remote village and is accepted by everyone. Similarly, in an organisation, leaders will not only rule the kingdom from the position of power but also the hearts of their people.

Therefore, Chanakya tells us, "There can be no country (village) without people. And no kingdom without the country." Understand this universal principle and become the leader among men.

NO ONE PUTS SALARY
ABOVE SECURITY

22

"Even for a very large sum of money, no one would
desire the loss of his life." (8.3.35)

Imagine this situation: You are stuck in poverty and struggling
financially. Someone comes along and tells you, "I will give
you a few billion rupees. In return, you must cut your head off
and give it to me." What would you do?

Any sane person will just laugh at the person and walk away.

Though desperately in need of money, one will not cut their
head off. An inner voice nudges, "If you are alive, you can make
the money that you require. What use is money if you won't
survive?"

This is precisely the point Chanakya is making. Even for an
enormous sum of money, one will not desire to lose one's life.

1. Life Is the Biggest Asset

Many assume that the greatest assets we possess are bank balance,
house, real estate, savings, and other investments. But it is all

gone once you are dead—you won't be around to enjoy it. Only the wise understand that the biggest asset is their life. We should be able to use it productively.

Once a very successful businessman hit upon bad times. He lost the wealth he had created, going from riches to rags. He was contemplating ending his life when he met a saint who said, "Remember, your wealth may be gone. But the person who owned the wealth is still there ..." This was a profound realisation: as long as he lived, the businessman could rebuild all he had lost, and that's exactly what he did.

2. Struggle Is Temporary

Every person has faced challenging times. But, ask yourself whether these struggles have ever been permanent. You eventually get over them. As you face them, however, the choices are clear: Either you end yourself in the face of the problem or face the problem and end it with hard work, strategy, and consistency.

Even after the darkest of nights, there will be sunrise. Struggle makes you strong, and winners never quit until they reach their goals.

3. Money Can Be Created

God created humans, and humans made money—a critical factor in all our lives. Chanakya takes this a step further: Everyone can be rich if they work in the right direction with the right strategy. If you are blessed with a mentor, guru, or guide, they will show you how to create wealth.

So, never let failures or the loss of money overpower you. So long as you are alive, you can rebuild anything you have lost.

WINNING EMPLOYEES: STRATEGY VS. TACTICS

23

"Strife among subjects can be averted by winning over the leaders among the subjects or by removal of the cause of strife." (8.4.18)

Human history has a long list of conflicts, disagreements, disputes, arguments, and wars. These have been a part of every culture and civilisation across the globe.

But, the leader is vital in ensuring that such conflicts do not continue forever. They must keep a check on these disputes. Instead of building walls, leaders should be able to build bridges. Instead of dividing people, they should inspire them to join hands for a common goal.

Therefore, in this above verse, Chanakya gives us practical guidance on resolving conflict among subjects. This is among his best advice on conflict management and resolution.

Here are the steps.

1. Discussion with People

It is essential to start with an open-minded discussion with the parties involved. Conflicts usually grow when the issues are not addressed at the right time. After all, a stitch in time saves nine. If there are any problems with someone, speak out.

This is also the first among Chanakya's four *Upayas* (conflict-resolution approaches): *sama* (conciliation), *daana* (compensation), *bheda* (trickery), and *danda* (use of force).

Sama, or "discussion," can bring surprising results. Initiating dialogue may be difficult, but only for a while. Once the ice is broken, it gets easier. If required, you may even ask a mediator or a common well-wisher to set up the initial meeting.

2. Winning Over Leaders

Here is an artful strategy to resolve conflict: identify the leaders of the fighting groups and gather them for a discussion. When you hold talks with several people, there is bound to be confusion and heated debates. The end result is what psychologists call "group polarisation," where groups tend to make more extreme decisions than the members would prefer. To avoid this, just focus on key persons and discuss the issue. Better to deal with the decision-makers—the leaders—rather than the many followers. Leaders are decision-makers. Once they are convinced, the others will follow. If they are not convinced, the conflict continues. They can make or break things.

3. Removal of Cause

Finally, one needs to crack the code. Be on the lookout for the core issue that caused the conflict. Often, it is not easy to find the core problem. It is often sidelined as more people join the conflict and bring their reasons to clash.

It requires applying your intellect and formulating a clear strategy to discover the core cause. This is also called "root cause analysis"—a valuable skill to develop as a leader. If you cannot find it yourself, take the help of experts. Their insights will inevitably help you find and solve the core problem permanently.

KEEPING MORALE UP IN THE FACE OF COMPETITION

24

"The conqueror, desirous of capturing the enemy's fortified town, should fill his own side with enthusiasm." (13.1.1)

A one-man army is a mythical being. After all, even the word "army" refers to a collective. The leader too will only be able to achieve his victory with the help of his team. So Chanakya guides the leader (those who want to be conquerors) to fill their armies (team) with enthusiasm. Only then will they be able to triumph over the enemy.

So, here are some steps to follow to become a great team leader.

1. Think Like a Leader

Leadership starts in the mind, and one needs to train it like a muscle. Unless you are convinced and thoroughly prepared, those working with you will also lack confidence. This is a game of strategy and planning. Unfortunately, many who become leaders do not know how to think like a leader.

Among various qualities given in the Arthashastra, the most essential method of thinking is *aanvikshiki*, or "strategic thought." Through rigorous rationality, inquiry, and exploration, it prepares the mind to face all situations practically and strategically to come out as a winner.

2. Study the Enemy

It is not enough to prepare yourself. Studying the competitor is equally crucial. Never take them for granted, no matter how weak they may appear. They could just have a strategic edge. To avoid being surprised on the battlefield—when it is too late—do not just study the enemy. Scrutinise their plans, modus operandi, thought process, and execution too.

This is where spies and informers enter. Chanakya had created a vast network of spies—both internal and external. The internal spies would gather information within the kingdom, while external spies would collect intel inside the enemy's kingdom.

3. Instill Enthusiasm in the Team

Once the attack plan is ready, raising morale within his team becomes the leader's next goal. Remember, armies are trained to kill the enemy. Yes, "trained to kill." To prepare someone to make such sacrifices is not easy—especially when it's their life. Therefore, morale is key.

There are many ways to increase morale. Be it "Har Har Mahadev," "Vetrivel, Veeravel," "Jai Hind," or "Vande Mataram," battle cries have been used to raise spirits for ages now. Not just soldiers but even the common man is filled with enthusiasm and a sense of patriotism as they are reminded of the cause for which they fight.

The other method is using music, often accompanied by instruments like drums, bells, pipes, etc. After all, it has been proven scientifically that music raises our energy levels, helping us "enter the zone."

Finally, Chanakya calls the one who increases the enthusiasm of his people *utsaha vardhaka*, or "the hortatory leader," who can overcome every obstacle.

KEEPING CHECK OF
YOUR PEOPLE

25

"He should establish [each] department with many heads and without permanency [of tenure of office]." (2.9.31)

Managing people in power, and thus maintaining a balance, is prudent. Any person, if they become all-powerful, can transform into a dictator. Given a chance, they could even destroy society. History is replete with examples of dictators bringing prosperous nations to ruin.

Therefore, Chanakya crafted a governance mechanism to prevent such outcomes. Several people work in the government. The officers and the various administrators have certain powers given to them. They are supposed to use it to benefit the people. Unfortunately, the nature of power corrupts them, and they misuse it for their own benefit.

Here's how Chanakya balances the scales in such a scenario.

1. Departmentalisation

There should be various departments in a government or organisation. Each must be assigned specific responsibilities, budgets, and other provisions to carry out their tasks. And finally, they must be given targets to achieve within stipulated periods.

In the interplay among these departments, they can either cooperate or compete. Their only option in such a scenario is to perform or fade into irrelevance. This benefits the kingdom or organisation in the long term. As time passes, only the efficient will remain; others will naturally be weeded out.

2. Various Heads

Never make one person the only head. There should be backup for every person, including the leader. For instance, a sports team will have a vice-captain *and* a captain. In case the captain cannot play the game, the vice-captain leads the team.

And no one in leadership positions should take their rank for granted. Many aspire to replace those at the top. There are only a few positions but many aspirants. Therefore, having different levels of power allows for a hierarchy that facilitates career growth and more leadership opportunities.

3. Do Not Make Anyone Permanent

The game is bigger than the player. Therefore, leaders should be made to retire when the time comes. Else, they may hog the position and prevent other, more capable people from taking over. As a result, we lose out on emerging talents and progress.

Therefore, see transfers, various postings, and deputations in well-run organisations. There are two benefits to this. First, you can have a variety of people in different roles from time to time. Second, it breaks the monotony.

Thus Chanakya ensures that he keeps a check on the powerful people in the system to ensure productivity and continuity.

THE VITAL TASK OF STOPPING ATTRITION

26

"He should favour those contented, with additional wealth and honour. He should propitiate with gifts and conciliation those who are discontented in order to make them contented." (1.13.16-17)

How do you keep your team members happy and productive? Chanakya recommends understanding the psychology of the team, which is often populated with different types of people, all with unique things that inspire them. An intelligent leader should learn what works for each.

So, he recommends four different methods to try with two types of groups.

Those who are contented should receive additional wealth and honour. Those discontented should receive gifts and counsel. Such measures will help curb attrition greatly.

Let us see how this works in practical situations.

1. Give Wealth and Honour

The contented group is also likely to be the most committed bunch. They should be taken care of, and the best way to appreciate them is by bestowing additional wealth. One effective method to do this is by offering them more incentives. This will validate their efforts and cheer them up.

More importantly, honour and respect outstanding contributors; as a result, their productivity will shoot up remarkably.

2. Give Gifts and Counsel

Many people, despite your best efforts, will not be contented. What should you do then? Chanakya recommends surprising them with material gifts and making them happy at the very least.

Once they feel appreciated, the next step is to offer training, mentoring, or counsel. This will help establish expectations, and they will discover how to improve and grow. This will also help quell any hidden frustration against the organisation.

3. Make Them Long-Term Players

People are a leader's greatest investments. They are the most critical assets of a kingdom, country, or organisation. Being long-time team members, they can also contribute with strategic inputs that help the organisation grow. They have been with you through ups and downs and deserve respect and rewards. The returns on this investment are immense in the long term, and everyone benefits.

BUILDING
RELATIONSHIPS

PARTNERSHIPS ARE FORGED AMONG EQUALS

"An equal should overreach, or help an equal." (7.7.12)

Chanakya asks, "What is life without friends, and what good are friends who only help you when pleaded with?"

If you have a friend and know that they are in trouble, reach out to them and ask if they need help.

This idea can be used even in modern-day geo-politics. We find countries allying with each other during good times but backing out during tough times—similarly in personal relationships. To avoid this and have good friends, first learn to be a good friend to others.

Think through these issues:

1. Who Is an Equal?

An equal is a person with whom you have the same status, ability, or rights. Granted, these commonalities can vary. For instance, you can be equal as friends in school, having shared the same space. Or you could be from the same neighbourhood, business, industry, community, or even economic strata. All of them should be considered as equals.

2. Why "Overreach"?

When you find someone who has hit upon difficult times, make sure you reach out. Even if, in the stress of the moment, they forget to communicate, you should not forget them.

Prolonged silence can cause relationships to fizzle out quickly. Make it a point to stay in constant touch with those in your circles. This could be in the form of meetings, events, or ceremonies, which bring us together and facilitate interaction. Therefore, leaders must also be good hosts and event planners.

3. Help Without Asking

Everyone has basic self-respect and dignity. Unfortunately, this sometimes works against them, never asking for help even in troubled times. If you know a friend is in trouble, do not sit idle; ask if they need help.

Help offered without being asked is real help. Remember the natural law—help someone during difficult times, and you shall be helped when you are in trouble yourself. Friends are meant to be there for each other, in times both good and bad.

JOIN THOSE HAVING A COMMON PURPOSE

28

"Being not restricted as to place and time and because of having a common purpose, allied troops are better than alien troops." (9.2.17)

We live in an age of collaboration. Competition is no longer essential to success. As a result, allies and friends have become more important than ever in the journey.

A shared purpose, bigger than the people, keeps teams together. Without it, even the best teams will collapse.

Chanakya shares important team-building advice here. Let's dive in.

1. Do Not Restrict Your Team to a Certain Geography or Time

A diverse team is a robust team. Allowing them to carry out tasks with flexibility is critical. This example fits especially well for the present generation, which is increasingly gravitating towards working from anywhere, at any time.

Once, geography and location would greatly restrict who you could hire. However, Chanakya advised seeking out like-minded individuals from far and wide to work with you. They may have to relocate, but everyone will be better off for it.

Today, however, you can work remotely, from home or someplace else, away from the office, and the meaning of the sutra is expanded accordingly. Flexible working conditions not only help with employee morale but there are also cost savings and other benefits. Moreover, the time and energy saved in commuting could boost overall productivity. So give your team members freedom and they will deliver.

2. Common Purpose

Freedom cannot be detached from responsibility. Responsible people understand that purpose keeps everyone together. It is the unifying factor, no matter how diverse the team.

As leaders, it is important to understand the common purpose and communicate it with those working with you. If there is no purpose yet, find it; this will define the organisation's culture. And, when you take on new members, only consider those who are aligned with the purpose. Else, there will be a mismatch and cause attrition problems. This purpose then becomes an organisation's culture, with everyone working towards the same goal.

3. Allied Troops vs. Alien Troops

Troops (teams) better aligned to the common purpose are crucial. Without them, productivity will suffer. Aligning your teams with a vision is a major exercise to undertake, but it increases productivity manifold. That is why companies spend a lot of time and money to train new recruits and orient them with both technical skills and the organisation's higher purpose. There are also new (alien) teams, especially in younger organisations. They start off unaligned with the purpose. While individual members may show great promise, they may not be able to collaborate when starting out. Several issues may crop up if this void is unaddressed.

CHOOSING THE RIGHT BUSINESS PARTNER

29

"If situated between two stronger kings, he should seek shelter with one capable of protecting him." (7.2.13)

Whom will you seek shelter with during a crisis—a strong or a weak person? Obviously, the stronger one, correct?

Now, what if you were to pick between two strong people to help you? Whom will you choose? Clearly, this decision requires some nuanced thinking. Chanakya has a solution. He says, "Pick the one who is capable of protecting you."

When these sutras were written, Chanakya was addressing such dilemmas in wartime. If you are attacked by two strong kings who want to take over, you must think critically and decide. Make a favourable pact or agreement when you cannot fight the war. Chanakya recommends the stronger among the two for your own protection.

Let us see how to apply Chanakya's wisdom in the modern-day setting using the example of a merger and acquisition.

First, imagine a struggling company, which is financially

weak and on the verge of closing. The leader likely holds it close to their heart. In an ideal situation, they would not like to sell their company. But here comes a chance to keep the company going: a larger organisation wants to take over. What should the leader do? Consider the following parameters:

1. What Are Your Values?

Consider your business' values—the principles and mission should not change drastically as ownership changes. This is especially important as pet projects usually have a lot of emotion and hopes pinned on them. Your employees too believe in these values, and it is likely that they'll feel alienated if these change.

2. Think of Your Customers

Your company's true north likely operates in line with the customer base you have built over time. If you wish to preserve the value you have created for them, partner with someone who respects and understands your market and vision.

3. Consider the Long-Term Scenario

Stephen Covey, in his book, *Seven Habits of Highly Effective People*, says "... you need to develop an emotional bank account." Similarly, feel things out before you jump into a merger, no matter how desperate you are for funds. At a rudimentary level, you could even consider this as a marriage: would you want to commit to a life of togetherness to only realise you have made a mistake a few months down the line, when it is too difficult to get out of it? Check with other sources on the potential partner and ensure you aren't walking into a room with a closet full of skeletons.

A CONSTANT ALLY

"One, that is protected and that protects out of
love, without [consideration of] money, with a
relationship grown since old times, is called
the constant ally." (7.9.39)

L ove and understanding are the foundation of friendship.
Without them, the relationship becomes transactional.
Therefore, we must look at the depth and discover those time-
tested relationships.

In Marathi, there is an adage, "*kama purta mama*," which
describes someone who acts like a relative but only for selfish
reasons. Otherwise, they are indifferent to your presence.
Naturally, no one likes such opportunists. Given a choice,
Chanakya advises avoiding them altogether.

Let us further explore this sutra to understand its depth. We
can even call this a checklist for genuine friends.

1. Ensure Reciprocation

A person who feels protected and protects you out of love is rare. However, like a stressed person cannot help another relax, those who do not find their feelings reciprocated will not come to your support. You should bring as much to the relationship as they do—in terms of resources or otherwise.

2. Not Money Minded

At the same time, the intentions should be right and not materialistic. Money is a strange thing. It makes the world go round. People who cling to you for monetary gain are merely dealers, not allies. Thankfully, it is easy to spot them before any real damage can be done. The early sign is usually of them growing bitter when you spurn their requests. Avoid them, and they will move on. You too must do the same.

3. The Best Relationships Are Time-Tested

The real test of friendship is time. The longer the association, the stronger it is. The reason for this is simple: longer relationships tend to see ups and downs. If you can stick together despite these fluctuations in life and business, you will likely share a long and fruitful relationship. Such is the quality of true allies in life: you are together, forever.

BRINGING OUT THE BEST IN YOUR "FRIENDS"

31

"Being constant—this is the excellence of an ally."
(6.1.12)

Confidence is your greatest asset when facing challenges. And the feeling that we are not alone instils the most confidence in us. Friends and allies fulfil this role in our lives— allowing us to face challenges head-on, assured of a safety net should anything go wrong. Chanakya recommends never fighting a battle alone. Always bring some friends along.

Let's examine these verses:

1. Being a Constant

But how does one recognise who is a good friend? Chanakya shares an important piece of advice here: "Being constant is the excellence of an ally (friend)."

Those who stick with us in good *and* bad times are genuine friends. Friendships face their actual test in the face of failure. You must avoid those who are inconsistent, like the wind's direction, weaving in when you are a success and dodging you when you're down. Such people are likely unstable in every relationship.

Similarly, be constant and consistent in all your friendships. Do not run away when your friend is in trouble. Help them with all your might and resources. If required to help this friend, enlist the support of other connections too.

2. Avoid Overdependence

On the topic of allies, Chanakya drops another hint: never have only one—have many. This will keep you from overdependence on anyone, thus protecting your interests should they betray you. Help everyone as often as possible, per your capacity and capability. Moreover, this expanded circle allows you to enlist the support of many.

KNOWING WHOM TO
APPROACH FOR SHELTER

32

"Those to whom he may be dear, or those who may be
dear to him—which one should he approach for shelter?"

More than advice, this sutra poses a thought-provoking
question that will train you to make the right decision
in a crisis. This is the scenario: you have run out of options and
have to escape and take shelter to save your life. It is a matter of
life and death. Whom will you take refuge with?

Let us consider this in detail.

1. To Whom He May Be Dear

Some in life will dislike us despite our best efforts to appease
them. Others, regardless of any special gesture on our part, will
like us. A parent's love for their child is much like this. You must
have already come across such situations and felt confused. In
such cases, recognise those who like you, to whom you may be
dear. Know them and be aware of their presence.

2. Who May Be Dear to Him

Now we consider the second category of people. Whom we consider dear to us. Come what may, we still love them. They are always at the top of our minds. We will do anything for them—no questions asked. We will even give up everything for them, including our lives, if needed.

Now, think about what you will do in such a situation before you flip to the next sutra for an answer.

KNOWING WHOM TO APPROACH FOR SHELTER

(Chanakya's reply—a continuation of the previous sutra.)

"He should go to him he may be dear to. This is the best course of seeking shelter." (7.2.25)

L ike any good teacher, Chanakya not only confuses but provides clarity. Moreover, as a philosophy and strategic thinking teacher, his response offers perspective along those lines.

Let us understand in detail the rationale behind the suggestion:

1. Whom to Approach?

For a detailed answer, you should read the original Arthashastra. Furthermore, there are many such situations, along with choices given by Chanakya, to choose from.

For now, however, I will share the brief answer with you.

Choose the first type of person: the one you are dear to.

The reason is simple. Just as you would do anything for those dear to you, if you are special to someone, they will go to any extent to protect you. Not necessarily so in the latter choice. You may like someone but not win their affection. They may even ditch you at the last moment when you need them most. So, be careful and intelligent in your approach towards others, warns Chanakya.

2. "Go" to Him

In the age of technology and fast communication, do not just send a message; talk to the person and try to meet them face-to-face. This will make a massive difference in the outcome.

THE DIFFERENT WAYS OF ACQUIRING A COMPANY

"Acquisition is of three kinds: new, formerly possessed, and inherited." (13.5.2)

This is a very relevant sutra for mature businesspeople, evolved companies, and strategic investors. After the growth stage, companies acquire smaller organisations to expand and capture new markets and clients. Chanakya shares three types of acquisitions that happen. This is not only applicable to business groups, but also individuals, various other organisations, and countries. This sutra is relevant in geopolitics too, when nations want to expand and acquire new lands and territories. Chanakya is guiding us here with three options.

1. New

There are two ways of acquiring new territories or lands. The negative way is by attacking another kingdom or nation. The positive way is by purchasing land. In the case of large companies, they buy out smaller companies or start-ups. It is a win-win situation for both. The bigger company saves on the time and energy it would have spent creating a new vertical or expanding. At the same time, the smaller organisation receives large sums from the large company that acquires them.

2. Formerly Possessed

Sometimes, one has to sell off some assets due to an unfavourable situation. However, one can repurchase those assets when the conditions improve. For example, suppose you had sold off some equity in your company for extra funds. This sort of distress selling may have been the best course of action in the given situation. But, when the tides turn, you can buy back those shares—if the current owner is willing to sell. However, be prepared to pay a higher price if the asset has appreciated in value.

3. Inherited

Those who inherit something are fortunate. In the Indian culture, it is generally considered a result of *punya*, or "merit," acquired in this or previous births. Businesspeople often inherit their parents' business or property, bank balances, and other assets. These should be received with humility and respect. There is a famous saying about inheritances that can help us stay humble: "We do not inherit the earth from our ancestors; we borrow it from our children."

CAREER GROWTH

DEGREES ALONE ARE
NOT ENOUGH

35

"One conversant with the science, but not experienced
in practical affairs, would come to grief in carrying out
undertakings." (1.8.25)

There is a misconception that education alone guarantees
a promising career. Many forget that it is just a starting
point—that we must go beyond degrees and formal courses to
be truly learned.

Chanakya's words are a warning. He is indicating that theory
is essential, no doubt. Still, those without practical application
and experience would become disheartened and put others
into trouble. The best example is Chanakya himself. He was
an outstanding student and a topper at Takshashila University.
He was also teaching there as an exemplary teacher. He even
wrote the Arthashastra. But his success was in putting theory
into practice.

Let us understand the same in-depth.

1. Conversant with Science

One should be well-versed in the subject they want to make their career in. Engage in conversations with good teachers and experienced people, and ensure your understanding of the theories is perfect.

Teaching is an ingenious way to reinforce your learning. In the ancient Indian *gurukul* system, seniors would teach juniors as part of their course syllabus. It helps you relearn the subject and revise it before training others. This also creates a strong bond between the students.

2. Experienced in Practical Affairs

Theory has to be put into practice. After all, the real test is when the rubber meets the road. Imagine a car being manufactured in a world-class factory. The design may look good, and the engine may be of superior quality. But only when it is driven on the road is it really tested.

Edison, the inventor of the electric bulb, failed a thousand times before he got it right. Likewise, in the initial stages, theoretical frameworks do not succeed. As with all experiments, they fail. But do not get disappointed. Instead, learn from your mistakes and move on. Refine your methods, and soon you will succeed.

3. Grief in Carrying Out Undertakings

Dr. Homi Bhabha was educated in England in the pre-independence era and was teaching as a professor at the Indian

Institute of Science. But his contributions were not limited to theory. He also created the first nuclear reactor in India, placing the country on the elite list of nuclear superpowers.

People who are only theoretically sound may come to grief if they cannot replicate their successes in the real world. Remember to always imagine the practical aspects of everything and plan ahead.

DO YOU HAVE "TWO" MANY BOSSES?

36

"They shall obey the orders of one who proposes what is beneficial to all." (3.10.39)"

What good is a leader who does not know how to take the right decisions? After all, many depend on these decisions.

Knowing this, one may wonder, "I am not the number one leader. All the decisions are made at the top. So, why should I worry and push myself? I better sit and relax. Let the decision come from the top, I will just follow the orders and enjoy my life."

This is narrow thinking. Though you may not be near the pyramid's top, you are still responsible for making decisions for the people below you.

1. They Shall Obey

There is no escape from the hierarchy of power. Be it a country, government, corporation, or private entity, bosses exist everywhere, and they expect compliance.

But the situation here is different: What if there are two bosses? Whom will you listen to? For example, you are working in a business house where two brothers are owners. If they give you conflicting orders, whom will you follow?

2. The Orders

First of all, understand what the orders are. Listen to them carefully and, with a quiet mind, analyse them. You will soon come to realise that the orders may be similar. There is no conflict at all. Why think too much when there is no controversy? Just act on the orders.

The difficulty arises when the two bosses make contradictory orders. For instance, one tells you to come to work on a Sunday as there is extra workload. The other asks you to take the day off, and just do the extra work on Monday or in the coming week. Now, you don't know which boss to follow.

3. Beneficial to All

Now weigh your options. The work has to be given priority. However, if the task is not pressing and there is no real benefit in working on Sunday, why do that? As a compromise, one can even complete the task on Saturday by working late to avoid an extra day of work.

If the work *must* be completed on a Sunday, there's no escape. Say, for example, you are working as a salesman, and an important client can only meet on a Sunday. Securing this sale could greatly improve your performance rating, and the company gains a critical client. In this case it may be wise to oblige the request. Seeing your dedication, you may even get promoted.

BE AN ASSET TO THE BOSS, NOT A THREAT

"Just as a serpent, lying in hiding, emits poison at the place from which it expects danger, so this king, having become apprehensive of harm [from you], will ere long emit the poison of anger at you." (1.14.8)

Relationships with powerful people are like a double-edged sword: they can make or break your life. Chanakya likens a leader's rage to a serpent's.

A serpent's poison can kill anyone it bites. It also uses the poison for self-protection against threats. The leader, therefore, wields his power like a serpent would use its poison: docile when unprovoked, lethal when in distress.

1. Serpent Lying in Hiding

Serpents or snakes are generally quiet creatures that one must try hard to spot. Unlike dogs and cows, which can be spotted easily, serpents lie hidden. They do not disturb you until you disturb or provoke them. So when people say, "I am afraid of snakes," it is actually the fear of the unknown. Remember, the snake is equally afraid of you. Do not disturb it, and all will be well. But, if you disturb it, it will try to use its power for self-protection. This is usually a very specific response—only the one who provokes gets bit.

2. King Apprehensive of Harm

The king or the leader's case is similar. They are generally found alongside close associates like family members, ministers, and other councillors and generally apprehensive of strangers. After all, everyone is vying for the position. The best example from the Puranas is King Indra. Whenever someone becomes a threat to his reign, he sends one of his associates to destroy the person.

3. Emits Poison of Anger

The king's immediate reaction is usually to get angry when he feels challenged. As in the case of Indra, he is likely to delegate the task of quelling the opposition to an associate. However, leaders must recognise that anger stems from insecurity. It is reactive in nature, and often illogical. If we apply a cool head and rationalise, it will disappear.

But, who would ask a person in power to cool off? Very few leaders are open to debates and discussion. The best course of action in this case is to leave them alone and avoid such situations altogether. Always keep a safe distance from the anger of a king or leader.

KNOWING HOW MUCH
MONEY TO ASK

"He should ask money of the rich according to their
wealth, or according to benefits [conferred on them], or
whatever they may offer of their own will." (5.2.35)

Remuneration is a tricky subject to tackle, whether it is salary,
capital funds for a business, donations for a cause, or (more
relevant to Chanakya's time) taxes in a kingdom. Chanakya's first
advice is not on the manner of asking. Instead, he asks of us to
study the person we will be asking money from.

Here's a breakdown of the types of people:

1. According to Their Wealth

Even among the rich, there are different categories: millionaires,
billionaires, and so on. These are called high net worth individuals
(HNIs) or even ultra-HNIs. Distinguish between these categories
and their purchasing power before placing your requirements.

2. Or According to Benefits Conferred on Them

A simple question to ask yourself when making the request is, *What benefit will he get by parting his money?* If you have an answer to this, there are good chances of your request being fulfilled. Everyone expects a return on their investment, after all.

That is why charitable institutions display the donors' names or confer awards and recognitions on such people. Similarly, in various universities and educational institutions across the world, endowment chairs are created in the name of funders and donors.

3. As Per Their Own Will

It may not always be possible to assign valuation to your work. If you ask too little, you lose. If you ask too much, you risk being chided for your greed. At such times, let conscience be the compass: let the person decide on an amount. You will be surprised by the sums they arrive at.

DO WE TAKE THE NEW JOB OR STICK ON?

39

"In case of two alternative routes, he should march in a region suitable to himself." (10.2.10)

Whether in choosing a career, changing jobs, selecting a life partner, or business dealings, we are all a product of the choices we make. However, in the face of hundreds of options, there is a trap: analysis paralysis. So, it is important to think clearly and keep a check on your strengths and weaknesses. To help us in the process, Chanakya offers a simple, effective decision-making flow.

1. Look Within

Consider your own response to the situation first and think critically. Do you feel you are doing the right thing? Does the choice align with your goals? Will it yield the best results for you? If you are unable to glean clear answers, or if you seek new directions, it is time to seek help externally.

2. Consult Others

If you are still in doubt, seek advice from other like-minded people. This external understanding will also help eliminate any biases that cloud your judgement. Another great group of people to approach are industry experts, who can offer foresight that you may lack. Chanakya too gives importance to experienced people who can guide and help you in the process.

3. Follow Your Gut

At the end of this analysis, follow what your heart and mind agree on—your gut feeling. Remember, this is not an irrational method. Emerging research shows that your gut-feel is likely informed by several factors, subjective and objective, which have been cultivated with experience.

However, differentiate this from the temptation to return to a state of comfort. Instead, be forward-looking if you want to evolve and stand out. In a sea of opportunities, few do this.

Finally, even if your decision proves challenging to execute, never regret it. March forth and make it work.

KAUTILYA'S ADVICE ON CHANGING JOBS

"One, conversant with the ways of the world, should seek service with a king, endowed with personal excellences and the excellences of material constituents, through such as dear and beneficial [to the king]." (5.4.1)

What is an ideal job? As one climbs through their career, one seeks higher responsibilities. One would like to work in positions of power, with powerful people, to become powerful themselves. At this stage, one should begin looking for the ideal job that utilises their full potential. However, this may not always mean switching organisations. It is entirely possible to transition within your existing company. Chanakya thus lays out a plan to approach leaders with such an offer, much in line with interview advice.

1. Gather Experience

Worldly experience sharpens your intellect. Spend your initial years learning with different people and understanding the industry's dealings. This experience will come in handy. Constantly refresh your knowledge and strive to move with the times. You do not want to approach the mantle with dated knowledge.

2. Create a Proposal and Approach the Leader

Once you know which leader you wish to work with, approach them with a proposal. Remember, not all key positions may be advertised. Moreover, such strategic positions could even be created to tap into a strong candidate's capability.

3. Make Sure You Know How You Can Contribute

Too many approach with proposals centred entirely around their accomplishments. They altogether forget that accomplishment is one thing, and impact is another. So, illustrate how you can leverage this past glory into returns for the leader you wish to work with. If possible, quantify this. All said and done, your legacy will be built on this impact.

DON'T FORGET THOSE WHO GOT YOU THE JOB!

"He should gratify, according to his power to help, one who has helped him." (7.16.17)

We have all arisen to our present stature with the help of others' contributions. So now, it is your duty to remember this support and return the favour. Even as we live in a dynamic world, we must learn to give back and keep the cycle of giving constant.

Here is what Chanakya advises you to do:

1. Remember Them

In the long run, we generally forget people and the things they have done for us. So list down the people who have helped you. Your first boss, the person who hired you, and those who mentored you—all of them are important pieces of the game. This is the most important document of your life. Keep updating it.

2. Stay in Touch

While this is just a touch away in this age, few *maintain* relationships. To make this easier, perhaps note down important dates in their lives and get in touch on those. This will afford you a good reason to call at least one–two times a year, sustaining the relationship.

3. Confer Gifts or, at the Very Least, Be Ready to Help

A gift is usually the most powerful medium to influence someone. Chanakya, however, advises against the risk of going overboard. Never give gifts that you cannot afford to, which is why he adds "according to his power". Instead, be thoughtful about it.

Gifting may seem superficial or unfeasible at times, so Chanakya offers a subtler route: be ready to help if they ask for it. This is perhaps the most valuable thing you can do for them. The HR head of a company said it best: "Always help others get jobs—you never know when you will need one."

MENTORING

GROWING IN THE SHADE OF A MENTOR

"Training and discipline are acquired by accepting
the authoritativeness of the teachers in the
respective fields." (1.5.6)

Many young entrepreneurs come to me for advice. They all have a common query: "What is the one thing that is essential to succeed in business and life?" and I have a standard response: "A mentor."

We always require the help of experienced people when taking up important projects. However, this should not be conflated with them deciding every detail of our execution process. A mentor experienced in the field, must merely direct, not command. Therefore, the best formula is a combination of freedom, training, self-discipline, and guidance.

Let us look at this in detail:

1. Training and Discipline

Every person who aspires to be successful must be trained to face challenges. When you invest your time, effort, and money on training and education, you are preparing for the future. However, this training is of no use without disciplined practice.

In the ancient Indian gurukul model, teachers would train the students in various subjects first and then put them through practical exercises. Acing those required tremendous discipline on the students' part, thus cultivating consistency.

2. Accepting Authoritativeness

Students must accept that the teacher is an authority on the subject, no matter how many ideas are brimming in the students' heads. The guidance may sometimes be difficult to follow. However, the path to follow is one of *shradhha* (faith) in the teacher. The best example is Bheeshma in the Mahabharata: the product of many mentors, including Parashuram and Indra, he acted like a sponge in the face of their advice. The result was a formidable commander and administrator.

There's a second lesson in this point: Mentors are an excellent resource to broaden your knowledge base too. Should you not know much about a given subject, you can always approach them to be guided in it. In Chanakya's times, they were called *Raja Rishis* (philosopher kings).

GETTING THE CORRECT ADVICE

"All undertakings should be preceded by consultation.
Holding a consultation with only one, he may not be
able to reach a decision in difficult matters. With
more councilors it is difficult to reach decisions and
maintain secrecy." (1.15.2,35,40)

Half the outcome of any undertaking is decided by how
you begin, and the best first step is to consult others. For
instance, the Mahabharata was not won by the Pandavas on the
18th or the last day of the war. It was won even before the war
started, the day both Arjuna and Duryodhana went to seek the
support and alliance of Krishna. Arjuna chose to have Krishna
on his side as an advisor, sealing the fate of the Kauravas.

This is the exact wisdom Chanakya gives us in the above
sutra. Pick your advisors and consultants very carefully in the
initial stages. They can make or break you.

Let us understand the sutra's essence:

1. Do Not Proceed Without Consulting

Have the humility to accept support in all your undertakings.

You do not, and cannot, know all. History is rife with examples of leaders who failed spectacularly after they were too haughty to consult others before beginning a new task. However, when we say consultants, it does not mean only professional paid consultants. It may as well be someone from your circle who is good in that subject or field. For instance, if you want to learn cooking, you can start by taking the advice of the best cook you know—perhaps your mother or grandmother. You will soon also realise that you make fewer mistakes when being guided.

2. Don't Have Just One Consultant

Remember not to overdepend on a single person to assist you in making your decision. The final outcome should always be a result of your own understanding and judgement, supplemented by the advice of multiple people, each of whom brings different perspectives to the table.

Continuing the cooking example, apart from learning from your mother or grandmother, you can also take tips from other folk you know who cook well. They may teach you something new, or offer a twist to a traditional recipe.

3. Don't Have too Many Consultants

However, do not overdo this. Getting too many people involved is often a recipe for confusion and complications. The adage "too many cooks spoil the broth" rings true in this case. Additionally, you risk having the information leaked if too many people get involved in decision-making, especially in the case of sensitive matters. Moderation is key. Take on only as much advice as you can assimilate and mull over. Consultants are like roadmaps, after all. They will show you the way, but you will still have to walk the path yourself.

WHOM TO TAKE ADVICE FROM

"Therefore, sit and counsel with those who are matured
in intellect." (1.15.20-21)

Chanakya then lays out the final course of action, having
selected guides for your task.

1. Sit Down and Take Counsel

In the Indian spiritual tradition, sitting down is considered a
mark of respect to others. When a disciple goes to meet his
teacher, the disciple must sit down and be face-to-face with the
teacher. The term "Upanishad" means to "sit next to (generally)
a wise person."

Sitting also denotes humility. Water always flows from
the higher level to the lower levels. In the similar manner,
knowledge flows from the teacher to the student. While a simple
instruction, it's significance is immense.

2. Matured in Intellect

The mentor, advisor, or counsellor should have this critical quality. Maturity is the state of being where the person is balanced mentally and emotionally and can deal with the situation at hand. If we are confused, we cannot have another confused person guiding us.

Also, they should be matured in intellect. Intelligence is the faculty of a person to think logically and rationally. It has to be based on facts and figures. Many so-called motivators make you feel good in a given moment but, when you think with a calm and quiet mind, you will realise their advice has no basis in reality. Avoid such people at all costs.

WANT TO BE A GOOD BOSS?
ASK YOUR DAD!

"And, in all cases, he should favour the stricken [subjects] like a father." (4.4.43)

People often don't quit organisations—they quit bosses. To be an ideal leader, however, often proves a challenge.

Chanakya, therefore, uses an example from the household: the role of a father or parent. They are ever loving and concerned for their children. They may be disciplinarians, but the attitude is always about care and concern.

Here are some tips you can adopt:

1. Understand Them

The king must deal with various cases every day and must handle it all with a sense of equanimity and poise. The first step in this is to empathise with people. In case of your employees, understand that they aren't merely there to make you a neat profit. They have their own families, friends, and interests. Tune in, understand their expectations and manage them. Get to the root of the issue.

2. Favour the Stricken

Unfortunate events come unannounced. Your employees may have hit upon a rough patch, causing a dip in their performance. This could be a range of things: from unfortunate events like the death of a family member, a health scare, and so on. In such situations, the leader should favour the employee. In fact, Chanakya would go one step further. Instead of the citizens or subjects waiting to approach him in such calamities, he would be proactive and approach them himself.

3. Discipline with Love

This is the greatest challenge for a leader. Chanakya recommends disciplining as a parent would, fairly and for good reason. Remember that direct experience is often the best teacher. Despite your best efforts, the employee may still make mistakes. Accept it with love and grace, and proceed to correct it. To avoid giving in to impulsive, reactionary methods and set up a framework that help underperforming or rebelling employees reconcile with the organisation's goals. Doing so also maintains a balance between discipline and love.

After all, a man learns that his father was right when his son tells him that he is wrong. Maybe we will need to remember this while dealing with our employees.

CONSTANT ASSOCIATION

46

"He should have constant association with elders in
learning for the sake of improving his training, since
training has its root in that." (1.5.11)

We all require training: right from the moment we are born
and attempt to walk, to getting educated and growing in
our professional life. Chanakya witnessed the power of training
firsthand: first in his own case, and later with Chandragupta, who
proved to be an excellent ruler.

Let us now see how he approaches this:

1. Constant Association with Elders

The first step is to have a good trainer, be it the guru, teacher,
coach, mentor, etc. They must be experienced, mature, and
adept at theory and practice—qualities you are more likely to
find in *vriddhas* (elders).

Be in constant and regular association with that trainer. See
the course through to its end, else it will not work, and you will
see no growth. There are bound to be challenges, but do not quit
when they come up.

2. Constant Practice

The person undergoing the training has an additional responsibility: to practice and continue learning when the trainer is not around. For instance, a student learning a musical instrument may be brilliant but only has classes once a week. If the student does not practice those lessons by themself during the week, they will progress rather slowly and never develop an independent style. The same goes for any learning endeavour.

3. Don't Let an Absence of an Elder Handicap You

There were two kinds of students under Dronacharya's tutelage in the Mahabharata. One was Arjuna, in constant touch with and learning directly from his teacher. The other was Eklavya, who never met Dronacharya, but continued learning by devoting himself to an image of his guru and constantly practising. We should learn from the qualities of both Arjuna and Eklavya and become good students ourselves: appreciating guidance but not letting the absence of an elder/mentor handicap us.

MIXING UP THE OLD AND THE NEW

"As between a newly arrived [army] and one that has come after a long march, the newly arrived would fight after learning about the region from others and being mixed with old troops." (8.5.4)

Chanakya the master strategist believes that it is always a combination of the old and new that brings us success. Old vs. new, young vs. old—their merits and demerits have been debated for ages. However, the solution is much more harmonious: it is a combination of both that paves the path forward.

He presents a situation: A war is ongoing. Troops are constantly being churned, one batch goes in; when they return to rest, the next take their place. New fighters are constantly added to the battlefield. The old fighters have garnered experience, but are weary from battle. The fresh platoon troop has energy but no experience. "Open up channels of communication between them and mix them to win the war," says Chanakya.

In an organisation, the older people are the experienced

soldiers. They know the lay of the land (the market and customers). The fresh hires are the newly-arrived army. They are energetic and eager to learn. The leader's task is to perceive this and help with the knowledge transfer.

Let us see how.

1. Encourage Open-Mindedness

The old-timers should be open to change and allow newer hires to implement their own processes as long as they align with the organisation's needs. Moreover, learn from them. They are well versed in modern tools—computers, the internet, and smartphones. This will go a long way in both helping them settle and breaking the ice between the generations.

2. Encourage an Atmosphere of Learning

On the other hand, the incoming people should appreciate the older generation's experience and imbibe lessons. The former may have drive and passion but lack the wisdom and maturity required to win the war. These only come with experience and guidance, so the new army has to learn from their seniors and be open to being mentored.

3. Mix and Match

Here is the solution: mix the old and the new employees and let there be open interaction among them. In the mixing of these two generations, we have the experienced seniors guiding the juniors. By and by, they will cover up each other's weaknesses and build their strengths. Together, they will become stronger and act as a complete team. An endearing story comes to mind that illustrates this.

Once, a business leader noticed that the school children were quite well-acquainted with the computers in their school. Those were the days when PCs had just made an appearance and were proving difficult to understand for his generation. He had a brainwave. He brought in the kids as computer teachers for his senior managers. Hence, the first computer gurus for his company were not corporate trainers, but school children.

TURN MANAGERS INTO LEADERS

48

"When he [prince] is ready for it [knowledge], experts should train him." (1.17.27)

Every generation has the advantage of the experience and wisdom of their forefathers. So, naturally, they improve on the previous generation's practices. But this is contingent on them being ready to receive learning and carry the baton. However, the onus isn't merely on the next generation. In the context of organisations, the human resources (HR) department plays a critical role in ensuring this: first, they must hire good people; next, they must train them to become good leaders. In a modern context, this takes on a lot more significance.

Remember, leadership is a mindset. You cannot expect everyone good at their jobs to take on important leadership positions. Therefore, the leader and the HR should keep an eye on those suited for a leadership role.

Let's break this down.

1. Wait for the Correct Time

Don't jump the gun on picking future leaders to mentor to succeed you. Allow them to settle in before making a move. Let them acclimatise, mature in the organisation, and watch how they perform. There are also traits to look out for, which the next sutra deals with.

2. Have Experts Train Them

Once you vet the candidates and settle on those ideal for elevated roles, ensure those with vast experience get in touch and train them. In modern organisations, this can be done using a mix of mentorship from senior leaders and continuous learning programs. The latter could be in the form of university courses, training programs, e-learning courses, etc.

3. Ensure the Learning Is a Mix of Theory and Practice

Sure, you can start by teaching the various theoretical frameworks and models of leadership. Kautilya's Arthashastra details many of these: *aanvikshiki* (logical thinking), *saptanga* (the seven elements of the state), *rajamandala* (foreign policy), etc. However, after learning these frameworks, Chanakya would train the potential leader in practical affairs to ensure the knowledge is well-rounded and doesn't fail in the face of real-world problems.

IDENTIFYING POTENTIAL LEADERS

**"He [king] should strive to give training
to the prince." (5.6.39)**

Every parent's primary responsibility is to give their children the best education. That way, even after you pass on, your work lives on through the prince (the future leader) in the making. Without training, even potential leaders will not become good leaders.

The word used is "strive" to give training. This means great efforts need to be put into training the prince or the future leader. We have already seen in the previous sutra that the best experts should be called to give the best training.

Let us understand what qualities to train a leader in:

1. Being a Perennial Learner

A good leader cannot be set in their ways. The first marker of someone ready to take on bigger roles is their ability to absorb information and then analyse and think critically about it.

2. Being Solution-Focused

A good measure of leadership potential is the person's ability to devise solutions, not just spot problems. Yes, seniors are typically the ones to come up with solutions. But real leadership potential lies in coming to the senior with not only problems but two or three potential solutions. Teaching this from an early stage also improves their leadership potential manifold.

3. Being Excellent Implementers

The best leaders don't merely plan. They can also get their hands dirty and play an active role in implementation. Sure, mistakes can be made, and their accountability increases drastically, but the experience is invaluable in the long term.

TRAINING CHILDREN TO BE SUCCESSFUL HEIRS

50

"For, like the piece of wood eaten by worms, the royal family, with its princes undisciplined, would break the moment it is attacked." (1.17.23)

The training thought follows from the above two sutras, specifically relating to parenting and family businesses. Chanakya warns about what would happen if the prince is not taught self-discipline. After all, children born with a silver spoon will hardly understand the previous generation's efforts to accrue wealth.

Chanakya likens such a family, with undisciplined children, to a rotten piece of wood. It may maintain a sturdy appearance but is hollowed from within. Barely any effort is needed before it crumbles. Therefore, it becomes critical to discipline heirs to maintain the integrity of the business.

But how can you do that?

1. Learn to Say "No"

In the prince's training in the Arthashastra, Chanakya uses two words to describe the end result: a *rajarishi* (philosopher-king) with *indriyajaya* (control over the senses).

When the parents are in a position of power, it is easy to accede to children's requests and fulfil them all. However, exercise caution: this will only cause them to grow entitled long-term. Entitlement is among the first signs of rot. Therefore, teach them to be disciplined with their wants.

2. Challenge Them

Play an active role in the intellectual development of your child. Feel free to counter ill-begotten thoughts and ideas while rewarding brilliance and critical thinking. The child will learn to step out of the box and their comfort zone and face real-world challenges. If they are in trouble, guide them — don't spoon-feed a solution. After all, a birdling only emerges after breaking out of the shell by itself.

3. Involve Them in the Business

When the time is right, start training the next generation to take over. Many successful business families practice this. However, avoid the trap of directly involving them in managerial matters. Help them start small and understand the realities of the business. Let them travel to and fro using public transport as any regular employee would. Have them report to someone other than you. Additionally, expose them to all aspects of the company. Only then will they learn to empathise as future leaders.

A multi-millionaire was driving in a deserted region with his wife and son. As they stopped at a petrol pump, the young son was asked to get off the car. The father gave the hotel address to the son and said, "Get here. We are going." The boy did not have any money or any sense of direction.

However, later, when he was a successful businessman, the boy recollected this experience as one of the best business lessons he had ever learnt—to find your own path.

RECRUITMENT AND REWARDS

MIGRATION: TO ACCEPT JOB SEEKERS OR NOT?

51

"And he should not allow in the city 'outsiders' who cause harm to the country. He should cast them out in the countryside or make them pay all the taxes." (2.4.32)

Seeking opportunities—be it economic or otherwise—is fundamentally human. In this sutra, Chanakya discusses migration from the government's perspective, and how those in power must handle it.

In most countries, "cities" are often the most developed and geared to give residents better economic opportunities. Among these, the so-called financial capitals offer some of the most lucrative opportunities for growth. Such places, be it New York or Mumbai, see high rates of migration. Chanakya recommends closely overseeing this process, ensuring that outsiders do not enter without valid permissions. Further, when they enter and begin residing in the place, the government must ensure that they are taxed appropriately.

Let us explore this further.

1. City Outsiders

Outsiders in a city can be of two types: those from the same nation but hailing from a different region, and those from other nations, seeking better opportunities. They may enter as groups or as individuals. But as the number of migrants starts growing, the problems begin—especially related to governance.

The outsiders also come with their families and carry cultural baggage. Even as they begin adapting to the new environment, they retain parts of their original culture. This mix, which is bound to happen, must be tackled sensitively and in a balanced manner by the local administration.

Likewise, in a business setting, companies must be prepared to manage employees from diverse backgrounds, ensuring a harmonious and inclusive work environment.

2. Residence in the Countryside

If migrants arrive in a city already full and bursting at its seams, their addition may cause more harm than good. In such cases, the city administration has two options: either to stop taking in more people or directing them to a different place. Chanakya suggests areas outside the cities or the countryside.

Such places are also cheaper to settle in. Moreover, they offer more flexibility and unclaimed opportunity. Redirecting them in this manner will help manage the population and avoid congestion. If handled well, such a move can help migrants get better quality of life for a fraction of the cost in cities. A good example of this involves real estate: larger houses in such areas cost less to live in than in If feasible, businesses can consider setting up branches or offices in less densely populated areas, tapping into local talent and easing the burden on other branches.

3. Tax Them

In case migrants do not prefer the villages or countryside, Chanakya offers another option: make them pay all the taxes. If they can afford the lifestyle of the city despite the high costs and barriers in place, they are likely earning well. Therefore, they can—and should—pay taxes appropriately and contribute to the economy.

In many developed countries, there is the concept of permanent residency (PR). The migrants, after a certain time, can apply for PR and they are allowed to be permanent residents of the new country. They have to pay all the required taxes. But, note that PR is not citizenship. They may not be able to get all voting rights in the government. Once the citizenship is also granted, the migration process is complete.

WELCOMING EX-WORKERS IF THEY WANT TO RETURN

"One deserting because of the master's fault and returning because of his virtue, [or] deserting because of the enemy's virtue and returning because of his fault, is one deserting and returning on good grounds, fit to be made peace with." (7.6.24)

L ife is strange, and change is its only constant. This also applies to the people in it—they are constantly changing. Some whom you expect to stay with you forever will leave you. On the contrary, those whom you expect to go, may stay forever. This is true of both your personal and professional life. As a leader, this is also true of your employees. Some leave and are gone forever. Others may leave and return, only to stay forever.

In this sutra, Chanakya considers situations where a leader must decide whether to welcome back an ex-employees if they want to return. Let us understand the situation from various dimensions. Chanakya wanted logic and rationality to rule over emotions while looking into these scenarios.

1. Master's Fault and His Virtue

We must first analyse why employees leave organisations in the first place. Such an open minded approach is essential to put the scenario in perspective. In many organisations, there is a formal exit interview process, where the outgoing employee can openly talk about their reasons for quitting.

Often, the major reason is the fault of the master or the boss. They may not have behaved in the right manner with the employee, and such matters must be considered seriously.

Additionally, the employee may have a virtue that is sought-after and which got them another job offer. Look into these aspects.

2. Enemy's Virtue and His Fault

Chanakya also considers a counter scenario here: when there is something good in the enemy, or the competitor, which the employee has considered while deciding the move. What are those virtues that you lack? Analyse. It could be better pay, friendlier work culture, or even more rewards and recognition for the employees.

However, also consider that the leaving employee is human and has weaknesses. If these can be managed, the leader can consider allowing it to pass. One cannot always be strict and forceful in dealing with employees; there also needs to be a human touch as well.

3. Welcome Them Back on Good Grounds

After considering the various scenarios and situations, if the employee wants to return, and has valid reasons for doing so, you should consider welcoming them. However, such a decisions must be made with a human touch and on solid grounds.

I know of many organisations where these situations are commonplace. However, it is advisable to not be rigid in such circumstances. The returning employees understand your company's value more and are therefore more dedicated and productive.

REWARD THE REVENUE CREATORS

"The king should put up with a minor offence and
be content even when the revenue is small; he should
honour with favours the officer who confers great benefit
[on the state]." (2.7.41)

Revenue or cash flow is critical for any state or business.
Without income, the organisation's resources may soon
dry up. Such an organisation—called a "sick company"—may
ultimately shut down if appropriate and timely action is not
taken.

Chanakya offers many solutions to turn around such sick
organisations and make them profitable. And herein lie the
tenets that helped him make India the richest country on the
planet. We can use these ideas and become rich once again.

Let us understand the process that Chanakya suggests.

1. Tolerate Minor Offences

Employees are humans, after all, and will naturally make
mistakes. We should be able to tolerate such minor errors or

offences. If leaders start firing every person who makes a small mistake, there will come a day when the organisation will have no one to work for them. Who will do the work then?

Chanakya suggests that the leader has to look at the people in his organisation the way a parent looks at their children. He has to be loving and caring as well. When children make small mistakes, we should be able to forgive and correct them. Thus, we will be like one big family, loving and caring for each other.

2. Be Content If the Revenue Is Small

You may not always meet performance targets. In such times, it is important to remember that ups and downs are a natural part of the journey. There could be external factors at play, affecting your revenues. Take a step back and analyse them.

Then, appreciate the team's efforts. Talk to them, inspire them, and support them instead of laying the blame on them. The outcome will surprise you. They will understand and put more efforts and perform even better. A happy leader creates a happy team.

Moreover, small revenue is better than no revenue. Feel content if the people in the organisation are working hard.

3.Honour High-Performing Employees with Favours

The tides are bound to turn. Your revenues could explode, making the organisation highly profitable. This could also cause a change in the leader's attitude. However, it is important to remember that when the team starts achieving targets and breaking sales records, you must share your financial success with them.

Moreover, we need to honour high-performing team members with favours. Rewards and recognition should be shown to the performers. In most organisations, we have revenue incentives or bonuses given to the high performers. Also remember to party and enjoy together when the success comes. This is how the organisation grows out of a downturn. In good and bad times, let all the team members be together.

RECOGNISE AND REWARD PRODUCTIVE PEOPLE

"In case more work is done than agreed upon, he shall
not make the effort vain." (8.14.11)

There are all types of people in an organisation—productive, highly productive, less productive, and non-productive. The leader's ultimate role is to understand this natural fact and inspire the people in the organisation towards its vision, objectives, and goals.

In this above sutra, Chanakya speaks about the case of a highly productive person in the organisation. Such people are rare assets. They work more than they are expected to, and Chanakya is suggesting that the extra work and the efforts they put in should not go in vain. The leader must recognise and reward them.

Let us see what Chanakya is trying to indicate:

1. Agreed-Upon Work

Every person in an organisation has been given a certain amount of work—what we call the "job profile." Look up any advertisement for a job vacancy, and you'll see the scope of work clearly defined. So this is agreed upon even before the person applies. In many cases, the wages for doing this work are also defined beforehand. After selection, these matters are set in stone. Usually, this process is done by the HR department.

2. More Work Is Done

There are some exceptionally smart people. They understand what work is expected from them and complete it before time. In fact, they need not be reminded about it either. They complete the work as expected or deliver it better and before time.

And in the time they save, they do more work. They do not wait for the next set of instructions. They complete today's work, plan for tomorrow's work, and even complete such undertakings in advance. Such people are called "proactive" workers. They are the truly super-productive people.

3. Efforts Should Be Recognised

The management should recognise these people. If not, they are bound to become frustrated. Soon, they will start asking, "Why should I work extra?" By and by, their productivity will drop. Their talent and confidence will fade away.

To avoid this, there are many ways we can give recognition to such assets. You don't have to start big—even a simple pat on the back, an encouraging word, or a small gift can make a person feel appreciated. Of course, you can also make it ceremonial, where you reward them. Setting up practices around accolades like "best performing employee" or bonuses and fast-track promotions for such excellent workers go a long way in building a good organisational culture.

DEVOTED PEOPLE SHOULD BE MADE PERMANENT

55

"Those who do not consume [the king's] goods and increase them in just ways, should be made permanent in their offices, being devoted to what is agreeable and beneficial to the king." (2.9.36)

Great teams run great organisations. The king would require a great team of ministers for effective management, administration, and growth of his kingdom. Therefore, selecting the right team of leaders is a big task by itself. Chanakya gives us many tips on the creation of effective teams.

Those who do not consume the king's goods—meaning those who are not corrupt or do not take away from the state treasury. But instead, they increase the revenue of the state treasury, and are the right team members and they should be made permanent (of course after due tests). Such people are devoted to the king and are beneficial to the kingdom.

Let us see this in more detail.

1. Those Who Do Not Consume the King's Goods

There is a famous saying, "The king's close circle is more powerful than the king." But who are these people? The ministers and the government officials who represent the king. Being the number one leader with a slew of responsibilities, the king may not be accessible at all times. As a result, it often falls on the shoulders of his closest aides to make decisions and run the show.

Unfortunately, as the saying goes, "Power corrupts, and absolute power corrupts absolutely." Many (if not all) such aides allow power to go to their heads. The king can avoid such corruption by only allowing into his inner circle those who adhere to high standards of ethics and morality. This way, the leader has assets around him.

2. Increase Revenue in Just Ways

One of the targets of high government officials is to increase the revenue for the state treasury. This is usually done through the collection of taxes and fines. But one cannot use wrong methods in this quest. "Achieve your targets, but never misuse the power given to you," is Chanakya's message.

Many harbour the false notion that one cannot increase revenue using just methods. For that to happen, the person's personal integrity matters. I personally know many leaders who are not corrupt, use the right means, and still are the most productive and efficient in their high positions.

3. Should Be Made Permanent as They Bring Benefits

Such rare gems in an organisation should be identified and made permanent. This process is a long-term but critical part of team and organisation building. Hire the right people, train them, empower them, and make them permanent by compensating them well, promoting them, and giving them bigger duties.

The leader of an organisation once told me, "I want to build a global empire. But for that to happen, I need good team members. Those who are highly productive and efficient without being corrupt or misusing their powers." His first task was to create an effective team that was principled, could collaborate, and become role models to each other. In the long run, he did create a global empire. The people around him were key in this rise.

HONOUR THOSE WITH GREAT QUALITIES

**"Men are to be honoured on account of excellence
in learning, intellect, valour, noble birth and deeds."**
(3.20.23)

There are different types of men. And they are classified as
per their qualities. These qualities in various people make
them stand out among others. In our great Indian culture, noble
persons with the highest virtues are called *Arya*. And such people
are respected across all strata of society.

Among all the qualities and virtues of great men, Chanakya
is pointing out a few of them here. They are, learning, intellect,
valour, noble birth, and actions (deeds). Persons with these
qualities should be honoured according to Chanakya. This is
one of the primary responsibilities of the leaders of a society. Let
us study this further.

1. Learning and Intellect

Learned people are the greatest assets of any country or society.
They engage in higher-level thinking, advancing a society's

understanding of our relationship with each other and the world around us. Without them, society will become too materialistic. Its lack of values and virtues, in turn, will produce a spiritually bankrupt world. A great example of such a thinker is R. Shamasastry, who discovered the original 2400-year-old manuscript of Kautilya's Arthashastra in 1905. This great Sanskrit scholar from the Oriental Research Institute, Mysore, also translated the Arthashastra into English, making it available for global scholars and thinkers. The king of Mysore during those days used to say, "The people in Mysore know me as their king. But the world knows about Mysore because of R. Shamasastry."

2. Valour

Valourous persons are brave, industrious, and inspire all around them. Society cannot progress without such people—they are the risk takers, constantly pushing the boundary of possibility. They prevent the human race from stagnating and becoming lazy.

A great example is Chhatrapati Shivaji Maharaj. By the age of 16, the brave warrior set about conquering nearby lands. He took risks and expanded the Maratha empire across the length and breadth of India. His strategies and policies made him one of the most unique and outstanding leaders of all times.

3. Noble Birth and Deeds

Being born in a noble family is a privilege. You get all the benefits of the family just by being part of it. Imagine you are born in a family of teachers. Both your parents are teachers in highly reputed educational institutions. As a child, you too will get the respect due to them and society will expect you to follow in their footsteps.

Clearly, being born in a noble family offers several benefits. However, this fortune should not be taken for granted. Instead of basking in the glory, you must remember that you're standing on the shoulders of giants and must carry forward the family legacy. It is like standing on the shoulders of the mighty. Your vision should be grander and nobler. Your deeds and action should be better and bigger than your ancestors. Swami Chinmayananda said, "What you have is their gift to you. What you do with what you have, is your gift to them." Let your family be proud of you.

TAKING CARE OF YOUR EMPLOYEES

"Not being rooted among the subjects, he becomes
easy to uproot." (8.2.18)

The roots form the foundation of the tree. If they are not strong and run shallow, they may not be able to support the tree, making it vulnerable to falling. Most of us look at the fruits but forget to see the unseen roots that support the tree.

Chanakya extends this analogy to leadership. He compares it to the people in the kingdom. He says if the king is not rooted or in touch with the subjects, he will be uprooted. This can be applied to the employees of an organisation as well.

Let us see how.

1. What Are Your Roots?

We should be able to ask ourselves, "What are your roots?" What are the foundations on which you stand and draw your inspiration from? The answer defines your personality. Is it education, family values, tradition, culture, or something else?

For the king (leader), the roots are his subjects (employees). Without the people, the king will never be in power. Chanakya says in the Arthashastra, "Without the country (villages), there is no kingdom. And without a kingdom, there is no king." The country depends on the people.

2. Priority One: Your Employees

The subjects (the people around you and those you lead) should be taken care of. Without them, there's very little to strive for. Now, let us apply the same in an organisation.

For a leader, employees are vital assets. Without them, the company has no standing. Therefore, there is a new mantra in the corporate world: "Employees first, customers next." Take care of your employees, and they will take care of the customers. Thus, the company will prosper.

3. Easy to Uproot

You make yourself vulnerable if you do not take care of your people. If they turn on you, you become weak and open to takeovers. Your own people, therefore, are your greatest threat *and* asset. When their discontent comes to a head, the leader's fall is guaranteed.

Studying world history, we will find a common thread—when people become unhappy with the leader, they throw them out of power and so starts the empire's fall. Similarly, empires with content people have soared. Therefore, a large part of leadership is managing people.

ABILITY AND CAPACITY
DETERMINE RANK

58

"From the capacity for doing work is the ability of
the person judged. And in accordance with the ability,
by suitably distributing rank among ministers and
assigning place time, and work to them, he should
appoint all the ministers." (1.8.28-29)

A capable leader understands the importance of a strong
team. Now, the question of good team-building practices
is a branch of study by itself. Chanakya deals with teamwork in
detail in the Arthashastra—right from the selection of the team,
and their training, to performance management. In the above
sutra, he gives us a concise understanding of this. He talks about
knowing the person's aptitude; based on that, we need to assign
them the right task. Further, real-world performance will give
the leader deep insights into refining designations and ranks.

Let us delve into this further.

1. Judging the Person's Capabilities

Every person is unique. Therefore, their capacity to handle work also varies. We find a simple example within families. Each member has a different task assigned to them in line with their capabilities: a member proficient at cooking may take on the responsibility of preparing food, while another helps keep the place clean, and so on. Together, their work supports the efficient functioning of the family.

How do we judge this, though? Start with small tasks and check if they can perform the task duty satisfactorily. Likewise, in many organisations, employees are given "pilot projects." This small task helps assess how well they can execute a given task; if they succeed, similar, more important projects are assigned to them.

2. Sustaining Their Performance

If someone is capable, why waste their abilities? Gradually add to their responsibilities, but also compensate them equally. Otherwise, the person will get frustrated and demotivated. From time to time, also give them promotions and higher designations to avoid stagnating talent.

3. Ensuring Flexibility

Not everything may pan out as you had initially planned. However, you can fix such mistakes efficiently by shuffling tasks. For instance, if you initially judged a person capable of handling one job but soon find they perform better with a different set of functions, transition them into a new role. The same logic applies to allowing them to handle more than one department if they are capable. This is similar to transferring high-level officers and ministers in a kingdom or giving them more territory to control.

EFFECTIVE PLANNING

DECISION-MAKING DEFINES
THE LEADER

"He should hear [at once] every urgent matter, [and] not put it off. An affair postponed becomes difficult to settle or even impossible to settle." (1.19.30)

Quick decisions have become essential in the fast-paced world we live in. As a leader, you must understand that much of the work can move ahead without your sign-off. If a subordinate comes to you with any matter requiring your oversight, address it immediately. If these decisions are postponed, they may pile up and hamper the organisation's functioning. However, avoid the trap of impulsive decisions. Listen, observe, and only then act.

So, how does one become a better decision-maker?

1. Become a Good Listener

The first crucial quality to cultivate is "listening." This will drastically improve your perception and help you understand the other person's viewpoint. In turn, this will foster empathy, allowing you to put yourself in the other person's position. However, exercise critical thought: understand what to listen to and what to filter out. This sort of *viveka* (the right understanding) also extends as a good time-management practice when there's a constant, heavy flow of information coming your way.

What may be urgent to the subordinate may not necessarily be urgent to you. And what may be urgent to you may not be so to the other.

2. Establish a Time Frame

Deadlines can serve as a good check on procrastination, which can be a dangerous habit. So give yourself enough time to think about the matter and the various possibilities, but make sure you adhere to the time frame committed. Else, theory will never meet practice. However, avoid the trap of creating unrealistic projections, which could negatively impact morale, if you fail to fulfil them.

3. Overcome the Fear of Making Mistakes

One of the main reasons people procrastinate is that fear paralyses them. They worry that the sky will fall unless they make the perfect decision. Remember, every child falls when they are learning to walk. Get over the fear of making mistakes so you can make timely decisions. In many cases, taking some action is better than no action at all.

GRABBING THE RIGHT OPPORTUNITY

"Time comes but once to a man waiting for an opportunity; that time is difficult for that man to get again when he wants to do his work." (5.6.31)

Swami Chinmayananda used to say, "When opportunity comes knocking, we are either out or sleeping in ..." Success, as they say, is 99 per cent hard work and 1 per cent luck—but when you do get lucky and have an opportunity to boost your growth significantly, capitalise on it. So, be vigilant—the right opportunity does not come often.

Let us understand this sutra in detail.

1. Recognising Opportunities

This takes experience. Spotting opportunities can take years of experience—not all are as good as they seem. Develop the knack to differentiate between the golden ticket and others that are just painted yellow. This is a slow, gradual process, but your task is cut out in the meantime—develop your knowledge of the trade so you understand what works and doesn't. Be willing to read and research and keep your ears glued to the pulse of the industry.

2. The Power of Saying No

Do not waste your energy on false positives. You will likely lose out unless you learn to say no to things that do not necessarily help you grow and only paint a pretty picture. Ask yourself the following questions:

- Is it genuinely profitable and scalable in the long term?
- Does it fit my values?

3. The Need to Act

Do not wait to act once you see your chance. Take the example of Starbucks. On a trip to Italy, founder Howard Schultz saw people flocking to cafes and espresso bars to catch up. At that time, such establishments were prominent in Europe but not the US. Seeing an opportunity, he grabbed it and started a company that is among the most valued today.

In this context, Swami Vivekananda's words resonate the most: "Awake, arise! Stop not till thy goal is reached." Once you have seen the opportunity, jump in and commit. Do not look back. Perform to the best of your abilities. Remember, wild success takes gruelling work to achieve.

THINK BEFORE YOU ATTACK

"If there is equal advancement in peace or war, he should
resist to peace." (7.2.1)

Chanakya was an excellent war strategist. He staunchly
believed excellent preparation during times of peace
was half the war won. However, this shrewd strategist was no
warmonger—he had no bloodlust. In fact, as far as it was feasible,
Chanakya preferred maintaining peace. This sutra is the perfect
example. War is the last resort: the destruction to life and
property is simply too much to ignore. Therefore, it is crucial to
evaluate the necessity of an all-out conflict before engaging in it.

In a corporate scenario, this could mean going on the
offensive against competitors. Such clashes often result in a loss
of face for all the parties involved and should be approached
carefully. Better still, avoid them altogether. But how do we
decide?

1. Understanding What You Will Lose

Evaluate the potential for loss before you undertake an offensive.
Don't fixate on monetary losses: the hidden costs of a full-blown

offensive are far-reaching, including a blow to morale, loss of time and energy, and the extreme stress during such periods, which has adverse long-term effects. An army officer put it beautifully: "What we build in ten years of preparation, we lose in one day of war."

2. Recognising What You Will Gain

Next, look at what you gain from the offensive. Is conflict the only way to get what we seek? Is it absolutely critical to get it? Is there a workaround that will help you achieve the same results?

Now, look at the potential for loss and gain. Will the conflict leave you better off, or will peace yield the same result? If there is equal advancement, go for peace and avoid conflict.

Better still, attempt to converse with the other party and arrive at a win-win that doesn't require escalation.

3. Time it Right

If you still deem a clash necessary, timing is critical. If the enemy is as strong as you, it would be foolish to attack them right away.

Just wait for the right opportunity. A great example of this was in 1970, when Field Marshal Sam Manekshaw decided to stay quiet for a year as matters were not in our favour. Instead, he invested in preparatory steps and engaged in all-out war against Pakistan towards the end of 1971. This is strategy in action.

THE ART OF CONDUCTING EFFECTIVE MEETINGS

"He should declare without loss of time what is in the king's interest." (5.4.11)

Meetings should lead to decisions, not roundabout discussions. As you climb the ladder, meetings may become a prominent yet unavoidable feature of your routine. Therefore, it is important to always bear in mind that they are a double-edged sword—they are either a waste of your time or a powerful tool to make solid decisions that positively impact the business.

So, how do you conduct effective meetings?

1. Have an Agenda

Remember that meetings can be a big drain on time spent actually doing things. Without an agenda, they can be quite akin to wandering in the forest with no clear path—you are bound to lose your way. The best meetings consider and respect the time of all the parties involved in them.

Therefore, prepare an agenda before calling a meeting. Then, communicate this agenda with your team so they can arrive prepared.

2. Start and End on Time

Have you ever found yourself waiting in the meeting room for someone to show up? Frustrating, isn't it? To avoid such situations, enforce strict start and end times for the meeting. Many tend to overlook the latter, but it is equally vital. Unless you know when the meeting must end, the conversation will follow a loose structure and accomplish very little.

3. Come to the Point—ASAP!

Tim Cook, the CEO of Apple, says, "The longer the meeting is, the less accomplished." Once the meeting has begun, avoid talking in circles and quickly get to the point. This ties strongly into the previous point: if you know the agenda, you are empowered to address it.

Also, don't spend too much time discussing the situation. Understand it, but create an action plan. There should always be something for you to do after the meeting concludes. Otherwise, little has been accomplished.

MAINTAINING SELF-DISCIPLINE IN THE OFFICE

"One doing whatever pleases him does not achieve anything." (7.11.35)

What is the secret of success? This is a common question asked by all who themselves aspire to be successful. The answer may vary from person to person, but in Chanakya's book, "self-discipline" takes the top spot. From time to time, you will have to do a job that you aren't the most excited about. Your ability to perform such tasks predicts how well you will do in your career.

Though this discipline can come from an external source initially—a strict boss, for instance—one must cultivate it internally as they climb the ladder. Chanakya shares how one can do this.

1. Planning Your Day

Most of us go through our day on impulse. The task at the top of our minds takes priority. However, such an approach may not be in our best interests; it breeds indiscipline.

Instead, plan your day in advance. The mental impact of this cannot be understated. Different approaches to productivity will instruct you in unique ways of planning your day, but the simplest tip is this: clear the most pressing tasks first. This way, even in the event of an unplanned item coming up, you will not lose any time.

2. Understanding Your Limitations

Do you get distracted at the drop of a hat? Do you tend to spend too much time fixated on unimportant details? The first step to correcting these negative habits is to identify them. Only then can you be aware and on the lookout for such tendencies when they arise. Next, tweak your working conditions so your limitations don't get the best of you. For example, do you find yourself browsing your phone in little chunks while you're supposed to be working? Start setting it aside during work hours, only to be used when absolutely necessary.

3. Seeking Help From a Mentor

The greatest advantage of a mentor for undisciplined folk is the added accountability. When you have someone to answer to for your progress, your actions start following the best course. Moreover, you can discuss things with them that you can't with a colleague or a manager. In the above example of spending too much time on your phone at work, would you be more comfortable approaching a mentor or your boss? For most, it will be the mentor, as they can understand you and give you unbiased advice from experience, especially with sticky tasks you do not enjoy.

START NOW, DON'T WAIT FOR A MAHURAT

"Having found a matter for consideration, he should not allow time to pass." (1.15.45)

L ife is a matter of choices. Moreover, how quickly a choice is made can make all the difference sometimes. Do not wait for the "golden opportunity"—a mythical beast; it may or may not arrive. As the saying goes, the best time to act on an opportunity was when it was booming. The next best time is now. Therefore, do not wait for a *mahurat* (an auspicious moment). After having considered a matter and established its importance, act now. Remember, the journey of a thousand miles begins with the first step, no matter where it is placed.

In these matters, a few tips from the Arthashastra remain timeless.

1. Begin or Regret

The first few steps are always the most difficult—you will find yourself riddled with doubt, lethargy, and a temptation to procrastinate. Therefore, the first course of action is to at least begin. A job started is a job half-done. The rest, you can figure out along the way. Over-analysis always leads to paralysis of thought and action. Don't let it drain your mental energy.

2. Plan

However, be wary of impulsive beginnings. They never end well. The endeavours of Muhammed bin Tughlaq are a great example of this. No matter how well-intentioned, the king always found himself in a slew of controversies owing to a lack of forethought. If nothing else, take a piece of paper—or a simple Word document—to plan the next few steps and arrive at a rational analysis of the course of action. When you give shape to your thoughts, have the end in your mind. The means will get all the easier.

3. When in Doubt, Consult an Expert

Indecisiveness can hamper your actions and thoughts. But its antithesis is consultation—especially from experts. Avoid people who say "It will not work" without giving the matter an iota of thought. Such negative energy must be avoided, especially at the start of anything worth following up on.

4. Work Out Your Plan, the Rest Will Follow

Get started. The minor details can follow once you are on the path. Do not spend too much time working out details that will make your plan picture perfect. An oversight with this approach is that life is rarely that cut-and-dry. Unforeseeable events are more than likely to occur, especially after you have begun. However, having once started, you are invested in the plan and readier than ever to invest more. The most powerful thing at this stage is the willingness to finish what you have already begun.

PLEASE DON'T WAIT TO TAKE THAT FIRST STEP

"One trusting in fate, being devoid of human endeavour, perishes, because he does not start undertakings or his undertakings have miscarried [failed]." (7.11.34)

An astrologer once told a man that he would win a lottery and become the wealthiest person on the planet. For years thereon, he waited and waited for this prophecy to come true. However, after many years of not winning, he confronted the astrologer about his prediction not coming true. He was asked by the astrologer, "Did you buy a lottery ticket?" The man replied, "No. You never told me to do that…"

Fate can never act in the absence of human endeavour. Chanakya, therefore, emphasised action on the part of the individual foremost. If opportunities do not knock on your doors, go knock on opportunities, door at least—you have a better chance of receiving anything at all! But how do you do that?

Let us understand this in detail,

1. Do Not Rely on Fate Alone; Know Your Strengths

What many call fate is often your strengths magnified with the lens of action. Therefore, before you go knocking on doors, introspect. Chanakya calls this *swadharma* (your innate capabilities). Getting dependent on fate solely is wrong. Allow your innate powers to act as well. Swami Chinmayananda too used to say, "What you meet in life is destiny. How you meet it, is self-effort."

Even in astrology, it is said that only one fourth of your life is dependent on fate. The remaining three-fourths is self-effort.

2. Tap Into the Right Resources

Market yourself and ensure the right people invest in your efforts. For this, it is important to first know who these right people are, and how they may be able to use your services. This may be a long and tiring process, but be steadfast. Nothing can stop a determined person, after all. If you can't fly, run. If you can't run, walk. If you can't walk, crawl. But keep moving towards your goal.

3. Be Clear About the Financials

Though the initial example looks at a lottery, remember that free lunches are extremely rare. Therefore, always be sure of the financials before you pitch yourself to potential investors. Work these things out beforehand so your dream journey doesn't crash due to miscalculated economics and energy. Getting your dream job or project is not enough — you should be able to deliver. Human endeavour reigns supreme in every scenario.

ALWAYS FINISH WHAT YOU HAVE STARTED

"Activity is that which brings about the accomplishment of works undertaken." (6.2.2)

Do you think you are hardworking and "active"?
Before you answer this question, understand the big difference between "busy work" and "productive work." The first kind involves doing tasks that make it appear that you are engaged; in reality, little is being accomplished. The latter kind is productive work that achieves something and moves you towards your goals.

Chanakya further adds that only completed work can be considered as activity. Unless there are results to show for it, you haven't really done much.

1. Define Your Goal

Do you know what you are working towards? Don't just pick a random target, though — be selective. Find out why you are embarking on the project in the first place. What are you supposed to achieve? This clarity will ensure you don't spend your time on fruitless projects. One well-backed goal-setting approach is SMART goals, which are specific, measurable (in terms of progress and output), achievable, realistic, and timely. I know of a person who used to manage over a hundred projects simultaneously and saw them all to completion. When I asked him in wonder how he could be that efficient, he replied, "I have systems and processes set up for all my projects. I have a good execution team. But, I am clear I do not take up any project that I cannot complete. And once taken up, accomplishment is my end goal." This is SMART goal-setting in action.

2. How Will You Do It?

Start with a roadmap, no matter how rudimentary, and estimate the resources that you will need along the way. Moreover, remember not to place too much emphasis on ensuring things are picture-perfect at this stage. Go as far as you can, and the road ahead will start getting clearer.

3. Focus On Results and Be Relentless in Achieving Them

Abigail Van Buren, a famous American writer, said, "Maturity is the ability of a person to stick with a job until it is finished." Once you have committed, march ahead and do not look back. The going may get tough from time to time, but do not lose hope.

I would also suggest that you read David Allen's *Getting Things Done* to dive deeper into the subject. It is a good guide for the modern generation.

MANAGING
WEALTH

MONEY IS A TOOL FOR WEALTH CREATION

Wealth is not only what is "with" you but also what is "in" you

"Be ever active in the management of the economy because the root of wealth is economic activity; inactivity brings material distress. Without an active policy, both current prosperity and future gains are destroyed."
(1.19.35, 36)

Earning money and creating wealth are two separate endeavours. Money is a form of wealth, and a powerful tool to create more of it. However, it is not the only form: our education, values, relationships are all a form of wealth that we tend to ignore. Therefore, wealth is not only what you have *with* you, but also what is *within* you. While money can be a powerful tool to drive wealth, the Arthashastra also emphasises that the qualities a person possesses are prime requirements.

Activity, therefore, is the root of wealth. Without active strategies, a constant flow of information, or affirmative action, no organisation can hope to be wealthy. Organisations and departments with lazy management will lose their wealth or, in the best case, stagnate.

If you already have wealth in abundance, do not become arrogant and lazy. In a world that is constantly on the move, begin identifying trends and get with the times. Else, you risk being sent to the graveyard of companies that failed to manage their wealth correctly: Kodak, which failed to see the digital camera revolution, and Xerox, which focused too much on copy machines despite inventing the PC, are prime examples.

On the contrary, look at the Tata group of companies. They constantly try to innovate, capitalising on and moving their wealth around. They have also built up considerable social capital and continue to help society rise.

YOU NEED ELEPHANTS TO CATCH ELEPHANTS

"The objective of any king [leader] or state [organisation]
is to create, expand, protect, and enjoy wealth."
"Just as elephants are needed to catch elephants, so does
one need wealth to capture more wealth." (9.4.27)

It is a given at this point that a leader must create wealth for
all the stakeholders and expand his business. He should never
be satisfied with stagnating. However, he must also protect this
wealth by taking appropriate measures when things look down.

Chanakya further adds, using the analogy of the elephant,
the importance of capital and how wealth creates more wealth.
You must have heard the modern version of this: only diamonds
cut diamonds.

But how can a leader achieve all this?

1. Constantly Inspect the Work

Employees need to be held accountable for everything they are
doing. Else, it breeds complacency. No organisation can grow

without an efficient push-and-pull system in place. Therefore, keep a close eye on what is going on within the company.

2. Closely Monitor Accounts

A leader should be fully aware of the flow of wealth. In book one of the Arthashastra, Chanakya lays down a clear time table for the kings: spend the first part of the day checking the accounts and managing financial affairs of the organisation. Do not get carried away by the day-to-day affairs and lose touch with the organisation's financial affairs.

3. Be Tight-Fisted, but Not Miserly

The modern start-ups ecosystem in India places emphasis on angel investors, venture capitalists, and other funding agents. They essentially pour in large sums to fund ideas they believe in and those that could pay dividends at a later day.

Extend this to an organisation, and the learning is this: start spending on resources—be it tech, personnel, new verticals, etc.—so the organisation can create more wealth. Keep looking for opportunities to invest—both inside and outside your company. Becoming too frugal in business is not always the best move as you risk falling behind as competitors pace ahead.

KAUTILYA'S ADVICE TO ENTREPRENEURS

"Wealth will slip away from the foolish person, who continuously consults the stars; for wealth is the star of wealth; what will the stars do? Capable men will certainly secure wealth at least after a hundred trails." (9.4.26)

Continuing the economic and wealth creation ideas and principles, Chanakya guides us further in managing wealth and adds nuance to his advice with warnings. No matter how rich you get, you risk losing it all if you do not have the smarts to keep yourself wealthy.

Let's look at this in more detail.

1. Relying Too Much on Predictions

In Chanakya's times, forecasting was primarily done by astrologers well-versed in the movement of planets and how they affected your life. He recognised that kings who grew too impatient about the future and began relying too much on astrologers and oracles could squander all they had. Why? Because they then become too concerned with the future—to a fault.

The modern-day leader is also empowered with several tools that forecast future trends. However, approach them with caution and take them with a grain of salt. Instead, let your hard work pave the way for the future.

2. Wealth Is the Star of Wealth

Chanakya reiterates that it is only money that brings in more money. Remember, the first generation of a wealthy lineage starts slow. As future generations take over, they have a solid base to build on. Be patient, pour efforts, and let time do the rest. Finally ...

3. Trust Yourself

This is the closest to a guarantee that Chanakya offers: if you are capable, have a strategy, and work hard, you will certainly secure wealth. This has been proven time and again, and should not be conflated for a cliché.

Do not grow frustrated, even after a hundred trials. Keep working on that next step towards your goal and approach failure with grace.

THE ROAD TO WEALTH GOES THROUGH THE COUNTRYSIDE

"Wealth and power comes from the countryside, which is
the source of all activities." (7.14.19)

The urban-rural divide was an important subject to consider
for Chanakya. In every decision he made, he would think
deeply about how it would affect those residing in the villages.
FMCG companies have followed in these footsteps in the
modern age, designing products that target the large chunk
of the population that lives there—estimated at nearly 64 per
cent! Large organisations like UltraTech Cement, Hindustan
Unilever, and Tata all now have corporate social responsibility
(CSR) projects specifically targeting rural populations and their
development.

But why would one do this? Put simply, it is the potential
for growth. The availability of raw materials coupled with a
large volume of potential customers makes rural development a
lucrative project. Be it for soft drinks, mobile phones, insurance,
or biscuits—all are engaged in reaching these areas and tapping
the growth potential.

Let's understand why:

1. Potential to Increase Commercial Activity

The wealth of a nation must constantly change hands. It must flow from one person to the next and from one geographical area to the other. Without this, growth stagnates, and the companies, which grow with the nation, begin seeing a slowdown. Moreover, the largely untapped markets in the countryside give them the impetus to act.

2. Nation Building

Remember, the rising tide lifts all boats. As more businesses invest in rural economies, employment increases, and so does the spending power. This, in turn, will help businesses, fetching them more customers to sell to. Moreover, you also play a crucial role in helping alleviate some of the problems of fellow citizens in the remote parts, thus helping advance the nation and building social capital along the way.

3. The Abundance of Resources and Labour

Chanakya identified rural areas as prime mobilisers of natural resources and labour. Accessing rural areas means gaining access to these resources.

Moreover, it ensures a good inflow of quality labour. Even today, a large part of the population that comes to work in major metros—be it Delhi, Mumbai, Bangalore, or elsewhere—are from rural areas. Developing them will only increase the calibre of workers and, in turn, help the organisation attract talent.

YOU CAN STRETCH THAT PROFIT MARGIN

"He should secure an undertaking requiring little expenditure and yielding large profit and get a special advantage." (7.13.31)

There is a theory in management called "profit maximisation". This means the ability to make maximum profits from the given resources. Also, there is a concept of "optimum utilisation" of resources. This requires a strategic bent of mind to understand and implement.

Chanakya clubbed these modern management theories in one sutra in the Arthashastra centuries ago.

Let us understand this in detail.

1. First, Budget Well

"What gets measured gets improved"—this forms the basis of stretching your profits. Unless you understand the project's actual requirements—time, manpower, raw materials, etc.— money is sure to bleed out. Therefore, begin by budgeting and, when you have a clearer picture, set aside a sum as a buffer as well. If necessary, seek help from a senior or a consultant.

2. Optimum Utilisation of Resources

Resources, be they capital or labour, must be correctly utilised to drive the most productivity and realise the best profits. This is helpful to both employees and employers, aiding the company get the most profit while preventing overworking employees.

Note that *full* utilisation of a resource may not always be *optimum* utilisation. For example, let's say you have a project that requires 100 work hours. However, in a bid to save time, you give a teammate only 50 hours to work on it. What do you think the result will be? A burnt-out resource and a shoddy job, even if they manage to complete it on time.

3. Profit Maximisation

The two points above tie in directly with this last: the most vital factor in any business's survival. By strategising to lower expenditure and increase the bottom line, you ensure that the company is growing in the best possible direction.

However, be wary of cutting corners in the quest to maximise profits. Do not cheap out on raw materials or labour, as such practices won't bode well in the long term.

THE ART OF DISCOVERING HIDDEN WEALTH

"What is lost, forgotten, and so on is income
from other sources." (2.15.9)

Have you experienced sudden windfall—an inheritance,
a maturing insurance policy, an investment you had
forgotten about, and so on? Such incidents are not unheard of.

What if I told you such stories are common in companies as
well? We account for several revenue streams: active (sales of
products and services) and passive (returns on investments, rental
leases, etc.). However, a third category exists: "wealth from other
sources." Sometimes, you receive money unexpectedly from a
source you weren't expecting at an equally unexpected time.
This too has to be accounted for and used in the organisation's
best interests.

However, these do not have to remain surprises. There are
ways you can scout for this income source.

1. Review Old Accounts

Modern life and work move at such blazing speeds that some things fall through the cracks. Therefore, it is beneficial to look back from time to time and take stock of the past.

One way to begin is by cleaning out your shelves of unwanted paperwork, but only after carefully examining each. Sifting through these, you may just find proof of money due to you.

Alternatively, sit with your accountant and ensure every paisa of your wealth is accounted for—especially if you have slow-accumulating opt-ins like EPF. Did you know as much as 58,000 crore has been lying unclaimed with the Employees' Provident Fund Organisation (EPFO)? Don't be a part of the statistic!

2. Follow Up On Old Payments

Every so often, a client may fail to pay on time. When, despite follow-ups, nothing budges, we tend to leave it be, especially if it is a small amount. Yet, we forget that many such leaks can amount to much. This may be a good chance to look back on these pending payments: follow up yourself or delegate it to someone, but do not give up—trying never hurts.

THE NEED TO HAVE LAND AS AN ALTERNATIVE ASSET

"Of the excellence of land, affording shelter is best."
(7.11.22)

Human beings have valued land for ages. We have fought for it and killed each other over it, often crossing borders to invade and expand territories and kingdoms. Clearly, the love for land is embedded deep within us. Chanakya recognised why and shared insights on picking land in detail in his work.

In this sutra, he points to land's greatest function: to provide shelter during tough times.

Now, how can one capitalise on this?

1. Consider Various Factors

Don't get carried away by the current price alone. There's a lot more to buying land: look at what experts think it will be worth in the future, the connectivity, the local community, availability of utilities, and other factors, including personal preferences.

2. Do Not Write Off Remote Locations

Almost everyone dreams of having a property in a metropolis. Yet, the outskirts are also worth considering—either as a second home or an investment. Remember, these properties quickly rise in value as the area develops, allowing you to profit. Moreover, they offer a change of pace over the city's bustle, allowing you an outlet if you are overwhelmed.

3. Consider Your Home as Financial Security

Remember the Hindi maxim, *"roti, kapda, aur makaan"*? This affirms that shelter is a fundamental need. After all, no one can predict how life will pan out. In times of financial insecurity, having a roof over one's head allows for a safe space to recoup and rebound. Moreover, the steady value it adds to your finances makes it an excellent last line of defence when the going gets tough.

LEARN TO KEEP PROPER ACCOUNTS

"If the [officer] does not deliver the income that
has accrued, does not pay the expenses put down
in writing, [or] denies the balance received—that is
misappropriation." (2.8.18)

In any organisation, there are different types of people working.
Some are efficient, some are lazy and unproductive, some are
corrupt, and others have a lot of honesty and integrity. Therefore,
as a leader, you need to have an insight into human nature to
deal with people. Remember, a small leak can sink a great ship.

Chanakya here gives us a prime trait of corrupt people who
misuse government funds: misappropriation. If the person
engages in misdirection about the income received and generated
for their own benefit, they must be reprimanded. But what are
these forms of misappropriation?

Let us find out.

1. Embezzling Cash

All the money paid to a representative of the organisation may not always reach the company account. What happens then? The officer in charge may pocket part of the sum. Other ways people often do this is by showing fictitious receipts for company expenses to be reimbursed or by showing cash sales as credit sales and pocketing the difference. To avoid this, it is vital to maintain a robust accounting system and checks on reimbursements. Ensure every part of the transaction—whether inbound or outbound—is verified.

2. Misappropriating Goods

Some may also take the goods meant to be sold to a customer for their personal use, thus slowly draining the company inventory. While it may be difficult to detect this, especially in larger organisations, robust inventory-keeping is an excellent measure of prevention. Do not let anything he unaccounted for.

3. Manipulating Accounts

The pressure to sell and meet targets is always there. As a result, there are numerous cases of employees, or even leaders, manipulating accounts to mislead their bosses or stakeholders. They may show higher profits than the actual, misleading you about the organisation's growth and the employee's performance. Here, too, maintaining proper accounts is critical to weed out such practices and ensure your balance sheet is healthy.

BUDGETING TO BUILD
FINANCIAL MUSCLE

"All undertakings are dependent first on the treasury.
Therefore, he [the leader] should look to
the treasury first." (2.8.1)

Chanakya was one of the most practical philosophers whom
you could come across, and the importance of budgeting
was not lost on him. A nation and an organisation both need a
solid financial foundation, and this is a key step.

Focus on the cash flow in good and bad times. The person
in charge of the finances (the CFO in the modern corporation)
should ensure they concentrate on increasing income and
reducing expenditure. Going one step further, they must also
forecast the company's financial health based on present and
past trends.

Here's how you can do it:

1. Reflect on Your Organisation's Goals

An organisation's goals may change over time. Companies may
choose a period of maintenance and survival during crisis, such

as the coronavirus pandemic. At other times, when the market is euphoric and customers are ready to pay, the company may choose to shift to a growth strategy. Naturally, the budgeting systems for both periods are starkly different. Sit with your core team and decide what your goals are so your budget can align with it.

2. Set Up Accounting Systems

Maintain a comprehensive system of accounting that tracks the daily, weekly, monthly, quarterly, and yearly expenditures and income. This allows the organisation to respond to the financial situation in real time, forecast future trends with reasonable accuracy, and finetune the overall strategy as needed. In fact, do so in minute detail.

3. Finally, Identify and Manage Your Expenses

Budgeting will only take you so far. Expense management is the next step. Identify your fixed costs of running the business (rent, utilities, tech subscriptions), variable expenses (commissions, labour costs, etc.), and one-time expenses. Understanding these factors benefits your budgeting plan directly.

KEEP REGULAR CHECK OF YOUR ACCOUNTS

"He [leader] should check the accounts for each day, group of five days [a week], fortnight, month, four months [quarterly], and a year." (2.7.30)"

One of the critical qualities of a leader is regular supervision. As we have already established, one of the key areas to be supervised is accounts.

But how should we implement such a comprehensive, play-by-play system of accounting? Here are some things you can consider.

1. Daily Accounting Tasks

Several companies in India now use Tally or a similar accounting software to maintain their accounts. These tools should be refreshed and updated daily. Transactions should be reviewed and reconciled so you have a strong sense of where the money went. Each of these transactions should be recorded and categorised as they happen. If we can form a daily habit like this, it will snowball and become the organisation's greatest asset.

2. Weekly, Monthly, and Quarterly Tasks

Every month (or week, if needed), mark a day in your calendar for a financial review with your team. Not everything can happen in real time. Sometimes, it may make sense to record payments you receive via cash or checks and deposit them on a weekly basis. You save on trips to the bank this way and keep the cash flow healthy.

Generating invoices for clients could also be considered as a weekly or monthly task. However, this must not be delayed any further. Remember, the transaction is still fresh in their minds, and they will be more likely to pay you on time as a result.

3. Annual Accounting Tasks

This is also the time to take stock of your company's performance and health and plan ahead. Prepare your year-end financial statements as the financial year comes to a close. In India, the financial year usually ends on March 31. This is the time to create consolidated statements, showing profit and loss, the cash flow, and balances. An audit is also a critical part of the annual accounting cycle, mandated by the government.

ATTITUDE OF A LEADER

"In the happiness of the subjects lies the benefit
of the king and in what is beneficial to the subjects
is his own benefit." (1.19.34)

If we were to pick one sutra from the 6,000 sutras of Kautilya's
Arthashastra as the essence of the book's teachings, this is it.
Chanakya defines the crux of his teachings. I would suggest you
memorise this sutra.

Chanakya never wanted to create a tyrant. Instead, he called
on rulers to keep the people happy at all times. Else, public
sentiment will come to a head and dethrone them. Leadership,
especially as a king, is a "perform or get out" role, so do not take
this for granted. Be on your toes and deliver the best results.
One way of thinking about this is like a parent: be happy in your
children's happiness.

1. Serve Your People

Serving the public requires the application of several management
tactics. Unless you can channel your authority in the right
manner and serve the public, discontent will breed and grow into

an uncontrollable beast. Keep your ear on the pulse of the public and solve their problems as they arise. When they are happy, you will also derive happiness through them.

2. Think Long-Term

Note the difference in the two Sanskrit words used here: *sukha* (happiness) and *hita* (benefit). All beneficial things may not give you immediate joy. Initially, policy changes may cause trouble. However, in the long run, it may prove beneficial. For example, an injection given by the doctor can be painful to the patient; it will hurt in the short term but alleviate the condition as time passes.

Thus, the leader should also focus on policies that will offer long-term benefits to the people. In this case, the citizens or employees must also remain patient with the change and judge results over time.

3. Be Grateful for a Chance to Serve

The leader receives many benefits owing to their position. For example, the president or head of state does not have to worry about their survival and comfort. They are offered to stay in a palatial house, have access to luxurious food, can travel at will, and are compensated handsomely. Acknowledge these benefits and practice gratitude. Doing so will keep you grounded even as you become more powerful.

WAGE SYSTEM: A BALANCED APPROACH

"A wage is for work done, not for what is not done."
(3.14.8)

As the industrial era rolled on, a lot of importance was given to workers and labour rights. Laws were made for the protection and benefit of the working class. There were union uprisings, and many people rose to political power across the globe by organising labour-friendly movements. No doubt, the rights and benefits of the workers have to be taken care of.

But what about employers? How were they to implement these with their own interest in mind? This is where Chanakya brings in a balanced approach. Employers too have the right to get work done for the wages or salaries they pay. No worker should be exploited. At the same time, the workers should also do their respective dutiesfor the salaries paid.

Let's understand this better.

1. What Should Employers Consider?

Before you pay wages, take into consideration the work done. After all, that is what you are paying for. Most modern organisations have systems in place to measure employee output and attendance for this very reason.

According to Kautilya, a commensurate deduction is only fair if a worker does not complete their duties. In the same vein, consider a situation where the employee is repeatedly unavailable at work or fails to meet quality standards. In that case, the employer has full liberty to give the job to another capable and willing person.

2. What Should Employees Consider?

The Arthashastra also offers a system that keeps employees from getting unfairly low wages and other forms of exploitation. In fact, Kautilya also set in place a system to punish employers who did not pay wages: *"In case of non-payment of the wage, the fine is twelve panas or five times the wage." (3.13.34)*

Further, if the employee is unwell, he also directs leaders to allow them to rest and recoup fully before rejoining.

3. How to Decide on a Fair Wage

What is the correct wage for the job? Understanding your industry and the standard pay for that role is critical in this case. Keep an eye on the compensation packages of competitors for the same roles and, at the very least, match them. Several countries mandate a minimum wage, which is the least an employer must pay for labour. Additional benefits or deductions, in line with the work done, come next in line for consideration.

THE IMPORTANCE OF PAYING TAXES ON TIME

79

"Those who do not pay fines and taxes take on themselves
the sins of those [kings] and the kings who do not bring
about well-being and security [take on themselves the
sins] of the subjects." (1.13.8)

In every country, the government machinery is run by taxes
collected from the people or the citizens. While taxes are
essential as revenue for the government, they are a way to spend
it back for the welfare of the people as well.

In Indian culture, we do not limit ourselves to only the
seen world. It is also about the other spiritual world as well. So
Chanakya talks about the sin incurred if you do not use the taxes
correctly. The citizens are supposed to pay the tax on time. If not,
they will incur sin. On the flip side, leaders will incur sin too if
they do not use the tax money for the people's welfare.

While much has been said about the leader's duty in creating
a welfare state, let's see how citizens can ensure they pay taxes
on time:

1. Do Not Consider Taxes as an Expense

Taxes help build the nation and fund civil operations. When you pay taxes, you are also funding welfare schemes that come in handy in times of need. From employment programs to concessions on daily needs, they are all funded by the money you pay the government. Healthcare and infrastructure projects are other categories that your taxes fund. Therefore, in a functioning system, taxes are not a burden and instead help the citizens.

2. Do Not Wait for the Last Moment

The volume of tax filings tends to peak near the deadline. In India, under normal conditions, this is March 31, the financial year's end. However, this practice puts you at a severe disadvantage. Planning your taxes and investments beforehand will ensure you aren't left with a gaping hole in your pocket and a sour taste.

3. Hire an Expert if Needed

The tax structure is always in flux. As a country's financial condition changes, the government may choose to increase or reduce the tax value. This can get overwhelming, especially in a fast-paced world. To illustrate this, many company owners still don't understand how the GST system works. Therefore, it may be wise to engage a tax expert so you can sail through the process without floundering.

THE RIGHT WAY OF COLLECTING FUNDS

80

"He [king] should take from the kingdom fruits
as they ripen, as from a garden; he should avoid the
unripe [fruit] that causes an uprising, for fear of
his own destruction." (5.2.70)

Next, Chanakya turns his attention to the government,
dictating how to collect taxes. He gives an analogy about
how the farmer collects fruits. The farmer will only pluck the
ripe fruits, and unripe fruits are left untouched until they are
ready. Similarly, the government should collect taxes only from
those who are wealthy and not from the poor. If not, the leader
will sow the seeds of discontent and kickstart the end of their
regime.

Let us look at this in detail.

1. Do Not Tax the Financially Insecure

A good farmer knows when the fruits are ripe for plucking.
Likewise, poor people, who can barely afford two square meals

a day, should not be made to pay taxes. If you do that, you will provoke their ire. Conversely, the king should help them rise and ensure they are benefited from welfare schemes so they can transform into tax-paying members of society. This is akin to protecting unripe fruits from infections and pests while nurturing them. This is where many leaders succeed or fail—only those who master this art will stay in power.

2. Tax the Rich

You may be familiar with the concept of tax brackets in India. The idea behind this is to redistribute wealth and ensure that taxes don't become a burden. The amount of taxes one pays should be directly proportional to the wealth they have. If taxes become a burden, more people will default on them, and negative sentiments against the government will rise. High or unfair taxes have played a pivotal role in several revolutions across the globe, including the French Revolution.

DUE DILIGENCE

PRACTISING TOTAL ALERTNESS

"He [leader] should constantly hold an inspection
of their works, men being inconstant in their minds."
(2.9.2-3)

Vigilance is critical in any organisation. The human mind,
after all, is strange, and we can rarely ever predict what
a person will do next. Chanakya gives us a simple formula
to ensure no deviant activities are carried out in this sutra:
constantly inspecting the work done. To make people aware of
the need for such measures, the Central Vigilance Commission
of India even celebrates Vigilance Awareness Week every year "to
fight corruption and ensure integrity in public administration."

Preceding this by many years, Chanakya's advice pertains
equally to leaders and employees. It is no use fretting over
competitors when the company's greatest threats are found
within.

But how can you do this as a leader?

1. Establish Expectations Clearly

Remember that employees function best when the task is clearly defined. The scope of work, the process, deadlines, etc., should be cleared up before you hand over the assignment. One time-tested framework is to set SMART goals, which stand for *specific, measurable, achievable, relevant, and time-bound*. Here too, you can further break larger projects into smaller, specific tasks that are also easier to monitor.

2. Review the Work-in-Progress Regularly

The person working and the supervisor should meet regularly and discuss the progress. This also allows for a feedback mechanism where errors and missteps can be identified and corrected before it is too late. Further, on the employee's part, whatever course correction has to be done should be done immediately so that no time is lost.

Many leaders also believe in conducting surprise checks, which keeps people alert and working even when no one is watching.

3. Allow Them to Self-Monitor

You can also enable your employees to self-monitor so they do not have the feeling of being watched by a "big brother." Help them create and maintain plans, manage checklists, and log their daily tasks. The employees, in turn, can report this to their manager. This will also help ensure that they are more involved. As a result, when deadlines are set, they can accurately predict how long it will take to complete any given assignment.

SELF PROTECTION

"And just as the king keeps a watch over others through secret agents, so should he, being self-possessed, guard himself against danger from others." (1.21.29)

The leader has to be watchful since they are also being watched. Also, a sense of subtle ego comes up when you are the centre of attraction for everyone. Here, carelessness can have a huge cost. History is replete with examples of leaders who were ousted because of their negligence. How to manage this high-pressure situation is explained here.

Let us understand in detail:

1. Keep a Watch On Others

Any country, organisation, or institution has formal and informal information systems. And this information system is the backbone of security. Spying and counter-spying are interesting games. Even the spy is aware that someone will be spying on them. Hence, they cannot afford to make any mistakes. These spies are the eyes and ears of the leader. Through the information gathered through them, he takes the required decisions. In a modern context, this role is fulfilled by internal and external information-gathering systems.

2. Be Self-Possessed

The pressure is forever mounting on a leader's head, but they must remain calm. Doing so will keep your judgement from being clouded and allow you to consider things objectively. Conversely, hot-headed leaders do more harm than good as they impulsively execute ill-fated steps when they see red.

3. Be Aware of Internal and External Dangers

The leadership position naturally brings in enemies, and many of these may be present among your ranks. Those jealous of your position or vying for it may attempt to erode your influence in the organisation. Keep an eye out for such elements while monitoring your external competition.

PROTECTING YOURSELF FROM THE ENEMIES

"The enemies should not come to know of his secret; he should, however, find out the weakness of the enemy. He should conceal, as a tortoise does his limbs, any limb of his own that may have become exposed." (1.15.60)

Business is getting increasingly complex as time passes. And with the rising competition, the market has become a battlefield. When you start your own business, you enter it and must fight. You can choose to be a small player or have ambitions to become a unicorn. In this atmosphere, corporate espionage is not uncommon.

Maintaining secrecy is critical as a result. While transparency and communicativeness are also important, it requires maturity to understand that some things should not be revealed until the time is right. Also, one should be alert that communication should be done only with deserving people and not just anyone.

Let's consider what you should do to protect yourself and the company.

1. Do Not Reveal Business Secrets

Your business is likely to be competitive because of a unique selling proposition—something that you have over others. While the general sense of it may be public, do not reveal the exact formulae that allow the competition to replicate it. If you give this away, you give away your USP (unique selling proposition). More importantly, do not stagnate. Instead, continue developing this strength and capitalise on it to the fullest.

2. Find Out the Enemy's Weakness

Always keep a close eye on the competition: no move or plan of theirs should slip under your radar. This is where the market intelligence team comes in. Not only do they help you pick up on forthcoming trends before everyone else, but they can also help you understand what the competition lacks. Once you know this, find out how to use this information to your advantage.

3. If Threatened, Withdraw

In this cat-and-mouse game of information, it is about who gets the information first about the other. What if the competition discovers a key business secret of yours? Chanakya's solution uses the analogy of a tortoise. Just like it withdraws into its shell when it is threatened, you too should withdraw and reflect if the vital areas of your business are exposed.

MAINTAIN SECRETS TO
AVOID ATTACKS

"To as many persons the lord of men [the leader]
communicates a secret; to so many does he become
subservient, being helpless by that act [of his]." (1.8.9)

The leader should know how to measure their words. Be
careful of what you speak. A single misplaced statement or
word could throw the organisation into crisis. Likewise, when the
leader communicates information on a critical project before it
is ready, they open the doors for competitors to swoop in sooner.

All projects in an organisation go through the stages of
conceptualisation, preparation, and delivery. You may have key
secrets to guard at each stage that only a leader knows. As more
and more people start learning of this, the chances of a leak
skyrocket.

But how does this affect the leader?

1. They Must Bend to the Other

When you reveal a secret to someone else, you are empowering
them with information. You now must rely on them to act in

your favour with it rather than use it against you. As a result, you open yourself to blackmail and must appease them so that their favours don't turn against you. In a way, the leader has thrown away control of the situation—something they should never do.

2. They Become Helpless

If the leader's secrets are out, they will be used by others who wish to get their work done through the leader. At this stage, the leader then becomes more preoccupied with playing defence when they should be executing. In this helplessness, you could be driven to take wrong decisions that impact not only you but the organisation.

Therefore, weigh your words. Like a tailor teaches the apprentice, "Measure twice, cut once." Kautilya had a reputation for upholding the tenets of this sutra to a *T*. His enemies had no clue what he would do next, but his next move would already be in motion. As a result, he became one of the most powerful people of his period who made even the most influential emperors bow.

THOSE IN POWER COULD BE CORRUPT

"Just as the fish moving inside water cannot be known when drinking water, even so officers appointed for carrying out works cannot be known when appropriating money." (2.9.33)

This is again one of the most quoted or misquoted sutras of Chanakya. He brings into focus the human psychology part here. He talks about the psyche of government officers and how they behave regarding public money.

Let's look at this in detail.

The analogy is about a fish in water. It is surrounded by water. So if the fish drinks from it, no one will ever come to know about it. Similar is the case with government officers. They are dealing with a lot of power and money. If they take away some portion of the money, no one will come to know about it.

1. Understanding Employees in Government

Since a fish lives in water, surrounded by it, you will almost never notice when it is drinking the water—the change in levels is too minute for you to perceive. Government officials and employees in critical roles in an organisation are in a similar position: they are surrounded by opportunities to siphon cash for themselves. This temptation is only human, but the prudent leader must recognise it and implement measures to ensure they do not act on it.

2. Understanding Which Roles are Most at Risk

Understanding which employee is most like the fish in the water is critical here. A joke goes, "There was a government officer who claimed, 'I have never taken a bribe in my life.' A fellow officer retorted, 'No one ever offered him a bribe!'" This presents an important point: not all positions are made equal—officers with administrative and executive powers are often more at risk of engaging in acts of misappropriation of funds. If they are principled and efficient, it is a blessing. If not, it is a disaster. Therefore, monitor them closely.

3. This Appropriation Is Often Stealthy

Given the privileged position of such employees and the large amounts that exchange hands in companies, you may not notice the discrepancy without a robust accounting system. Even so, they may have mastered the art of hiding their tracks.

I once heard a government official saying, "Chanakya has said thousands of years ago about fish drinking water and government officers taking money in the system. We cannot prove him wrong." He is misquoting Chanakya. Instead of encouraging such officials, this sutra allows the leader to identify such elements.

INTENTIONS OF POWERFUL
PEOPLE CANNOT BE KNOWN

"It is possible to know even the path of the birds
flying in the sky, but not the ways of officers with their
intentions concealed." (2.9.34)

The idea of corrupt officers in the government continues
here in this sutra. However, this time the analogy is of a
bird.

Again let us look at this in detail.

1. The Flight Path of Birds and Human Psychology

To the layperson, it is almost impossible to know the path of
birds. But this may be possible for a person who has studied birds
(like an ornithologist) and is an expert.

Therefore, we can trace the path of a bird's flight with
reasonable accuracy, but the ways of officers may be challenging
to figure out, especially if they are trying to hide something.
Humans are incredibly creative, and it may be a task to determine
wrongdoing. However, it is difficult, not *impossible*. The leader,

in this case, has to be a keen student of human psychology in the context of the organisation's systems.

2. Assess the Risks and Offset Them

Is a person allowed too much influence in the organisation? Are power checks virtually absent for one party while everyone under them is scrutinised? Do they deal with sensitive information or assets? In such cases, temptation is bound to creep in. Unless the leader can assess the risk and put in countermeasures, they may end up with a problematic situation.

3. Act the Moment You Fnd Discrepancies

Since concealed intentions are hard to discover, alertness is critical. Make a preliminary investigation when you find a discrepancy or suspicious activity. No one will readily admit to being corrupt. Have you ever heard a thief admitting that he is a thief? Unless he is caught and pressured, the person continues to defend himself and prove that he is a clean, ethical person.

Again if caught, the person will conceal himself. He will become defensive and take measures to cover his tracks. There have been many cases when the most innocent-looking person turns out to have a criminal mindset or is the master planner of the crime. Here, we are not suggesting that you doubt all innocent-looking people, but be aware that criminals wear different masks. And we should be wise to unmask them the moment an opportunity arises.

DEALERS IN MONEY COULD BE OFFENDERS

"Just as it is not possible not to taste honey or poison placed on the surface of the tongue, even so, it is not possible for one dealing with the money of the king not to taste the money, however small a quantity." (2.9.32)

The topic of corrupt people in power continues — this time, with the analogy of taste.

When honey is placed on a person's tongue, they are bound to taste it. He will not be able to say, "I don't know how the honey tastes." The same goes for poison: it is the nature of the tongue to taste.

Likewise, people dealing with the king's money and power will taste it too, even if it is a small amount.

But why is this important?

1. The Possibility of Becoming Enamoured

Once officials have a feel for the power and the immense wealth associated with it, they may end up obsessed with it. If cornered, or out of greed, they may also exercise their limited control in one way or the other. Even a clerk—at the lowest rung of the ladder—has some power, which they may want to use or show off in front of others.

2. The Beginning of Greed and Corruption

The people who deal with such power and money are of two kinds: those who use it for the execution of their duties and others who siphon it to fill their coffers. Let's use a classic example: suppose a bridge or road is to be constructed for public use, and a budget is allocated. Next, government officials invite tenders. It is not unheard of that those approving these tenders may take on bribes to favour one contractor over another.

Chanakya introduced a check and balance system to keep an eye on government officials. He would have a regular audit of accounts and seek feedback for the work carried out from those who benefited from it. Eventually, the truth would come out, wrongdoings would be identified, and the perpetrators punished and eliminated from the system.

SILENT PUNISHMENT

88

"He [king] should employ 'silent punishment' towards
his own part or that of the enemy, without hesitation,
being possessed of forbearance in respect of the future
and the present." (5.1.57)

The king has the power to punish, and therefore should know
how to use it wisely. They keep everything under control by
setting an example with the right punishment. Chanakya is an
expert in this art and recommends various modes of disciplining
in the Arthashastra. The Arthashastra is also called *Danda Niti*
as a result, which translates to "policies for punishment."

One of the types of punishments he advocates is "silent
punishment," which may be apt in certain cases.

Let's understand this better.

1. When Should Silent Punishment Be Used?

Where the punished person knows and feels the pain, having
erred unknowingly, it may not be necessary to make an example
out of them. It is said that "The greatest wars are won without
lifting the sword." The same goes for the art of punishment. The
person is disciplined, and their reputation is spared. However,

one can take this a few steps forward and apply silent penalties with enemies, especially when the situation doesn't call for an all-out conflict.

2. How Can You Use Silent Punishments?

One mode of silent punishment in modern organisations is a silent, temporary demotion. By placing the offender on probation after a transgression, you assert that the behaviour is unwelcome without losing staff and putting yourself at a disadvantage.

Likewise, conflict has also evolved on the global stage—wars are now fought via trade wars, economic manipulation, and online. A prime example is India's push to reduce its reliance on Chinese imports and the US sanctions on countries that go against its values. This is also called soft power—the use of economy and culture to influence the other. Use them smartly and defeat the enemy.

3. Do Not Hesitate—It's a Matter of the Future and the Present

Do not put off the punishment, however. Dole it out. This will benefit the future as well as the present. It will prevent such transgressions in the future and help reform the offender in the present.

Punishments are essential in bigger institutions like government and state establishments and social institutions like families and educational institutions. Elsewhere, Chanakya also mentions parenting advice in line with this: children, if not disciplined when unruly, will not grow to become responsible citizens.

CRIME PLANNERS ARE MORE ACCOUNTABLE THAN CRIME DOERS

"He who causes another to commit an act of force saying 'I shall accept responsibility' shall be punished doubly."
(3.17.11)

B ehind every crime, there are criminals. Behind these criminals, there is often a mastermind. They may be working with each other with assigned roles—one does the planning while the other executes. Usually, the crime planners are behind the scenes and make the other person carry out the crime like a remote control. These people are to be punished even more as they are often the source of the rot. Curbing their actions is a sure-shot way of restoring balance.

Chanakya offers insight into tackling this.

1. Take a Top-Down Approach First

Look at the broader issue: what gave rise to the crime or transgression in the first place? In society, this means understanding the root causes of the crime: poverty, extremism, misinformation, and other factors that feed into the crime rate. Likewise, in organisations, factors could include weak monitoring systems and supervision, inadequate compensation, discontent with the leadership, etc.

2. Look for the Mastermind

These people can be tricky to find, as they can also manipulate those executing the plan to accept all the blame. A classic case involves a mid-level manager who was asked to sign some papers regarding an international trade deal by his superiors. Had he not read the agreement's details, he wouldn't have realised he was being asked to sign some dubious papers. He would have been responsible for the crime if caught by government agencies. He was forced to sign the papers, but he refused and saved himself.

Therefore, look into the details and find everything about how the crime was committed before you decide on a punishment.

3. Punish the Mastermind—Doubly So

If such folk are left scot-free, their pattern will continue, and others will be dragged into their vortex of wrongdoing. They are criminals who also get others into the crime world. Therefore, they are at the root of the whole issue.

CALLING ANOTHER A THIEF

90

"For one calling another, who is not a thief, a thief,
the punishment shall be that of a thief, also for one
hiding a thief." (4.8.6)

Everyone deserves respect. You cannot call anyone a thief
without evidence, as it carries serious implications.
Chanakya considers this act of defamation a grave offence.

Likewise, if you hide a thief, you support the thief, thus
becoming a thief yourself. Such legal and social laws have been
clearly documented in the Arthashastra to ensure that anti-social
elements don't cross their limits.

1. Defaming Another

Theft can be of many types: you can rob someone of their right
to live by taking their life, their social status by spreading lies,
and their privacy by spying on them, etc. You may even rob an
organisation by not doing the job you're paid to, also called "time
theft."

While prosecuting a thief needs proof, labelling another

"thief" is fairly easy: simply register a false complaint or spread a rumour. The public, or other employees, are likely to judge even the innocent man and declare him anti-social before the court or investigating body can pass a judgement. Therefore, such defamation is a grave act.

2. Be Unrelenting in Punishing Them

Allowing such acts of defamation to go scot-free validates their actions. Chanakya warns against this. Instead, he prescribes punishment equal to that of a thief for them. Such punishment will deter false complaints and ensure that energy and resources are not wasted on lies.

3. You Implicate Yourself by Hiding a Thief

Hiding a thief is equal to indirectly supporting the act of thieving. You become part of the thief's team and are responsible for the theft. As a result, you too will be given the thief's punishment. However, one should also consider whether the action was deliberate and allow concession if the person who hid them was unaware of the other's actions. Chanakya reminds, "Too much punishment can turn the king into a terror. Mild punishment causes the leader to be taken lightly. Just punishment gives them honour and respect by others."

THERE'S A VERY THIN LINE BETWEEN PEACE AND WAR

"For, when the gain is equal there should be peace, when unequal war is considered desirable" (7.8.34)

In matters of all-out conflicts, one has to consider various scenarios before launching an offensive. Even when provoked, it is important to look at all avenues before taking drastic steps, whether in an organisation or a nation. This matter often comes under "risk management" in business studies, and Chanakya's advice rings true. If there is a win-win situation you can work out, consider peace. However, if you are on the receiving end in an unequal scenario, prepare for conflict.

Let us understand it in detail.

1. Punish When Necessary

Remember that punishment is not dispensable. It is an important deterrent that fosters harmony and discipline in society. If wrongdoings were to go unpunished, their rate would only increase, which is undesirable to all. At times, however, conflict or punishment is the only route one can take.

2. Consider Your Options First

In the tradition of *sama, dana, danda, bheda,* first try negotiations. Find out how—and if—the matter can be resolved peacefully. Understand the situation perfectly well. If you still find the situation to be unfair, you may resort to an all-out conflict.

Taking the example of the Mahabharata, Krishna was the first person who wanted to resolve the conflict between the Pandavas and Kauravas. Many discussions were held. Even seniors and elders were involved. Krishna also went as a *shanti doot,* or "peace ambassador," to the Kauravas as a last resort. But when nothing worked and Duryodhana was adamant, the Mahabharata war had to take place.

3. Decide and Commit to Action

Once they had committed to it, there was no stopping Krishna and the Pandavas. Our actions follow a similar pattern. Do not keep changing your mind or delaying action, as the rift may only grow wider. Some agreements, after all, take more muscle than others.

WINNING OVER FRIENDS
AND FOES

"He should win over those of them who are friendly with conciliation and gifts, those hostile through dissensions and force." (11.1.3)

This sutra is quite popular in Indian society. Many even consider this the most important and practical aspect of Chanakya Neeti. It is called the four-fold method of getting things done, which was mentioned in the previous sutra: *sama, dana, danda and bheda*.

These strategies are used in different scenarios, understanding and using human psychology. This can be broadly divided into two dealings: with friends and with enemies (or those hostile towards you).

Let us understand these ideas.

1. Winning Over People

First, attempt conciliation, or *sama*. If you want to win over a person, engage with them positively: by praising them, figuring out commonalities, and helping each other grow, by sharing advice, or resources. Treat them with respect and hear them out. You can be a winner easily. As a diplomat rightly pointed out, "Behind every one war you see, there are 99 wars that have been avoided by discussions."

Not all may be appeased by *sama* alone; the joy of receiving material gifts is very much a factor still. Therefore, the next step could be *dana*, where you offer gifts to the other person to win them over. This may also be used to quell an adversary sometimes, winning their favour and buying yourself time. In international relations too, gifts are exchanged between heads of states. Doing so keeps the bonds strong.

2. Dealing with Adversaries and Enemies

Others can be tough nuts to crack. But before you escalate the situation, Chanakya offers a crafty penultimate step: *bheda*, or the use of trickery.

Remember the British policy of "divide and rule"? This is a classic case of manipulation to get one's ways. As the opposite party is caught up in infighting, you benefit.

Finally, when nothing works, Chanakya prescribes *danda*, or "taking up arms." This may be a tough call to make, but having gone through this hierarchy of action, you may rest easy knowing that it was the best option.

WHEN THE KING IS IN DANGER, THE MINISTER SHOULD PROTECT HIM

"The minister should take steps in case of a calamity of the king." (5.6.1)

Every person at the top has an adviser or second-in-command. They are vital as such aides offer respite when the leader is occupied with some other work. For example, when the principal is on holiday, the vice principal becomes the acting principal—the same is true in different leadership positions.

Likewise, the minister is the second in charge of a king and plays the same role deputies to a manager play in an organisation. However, how can one act on this advice?

Let us understand this in detail.

1. Observe the Leader

Don't merely follow the leader of your organisation. Actively watch and understand the *whats*, *whys*, *hows*, and *whens* of their actions. More importantly, try to read between the lines. Do not take the actions at face value. Sometimes, prudent decisions are wrought from years of experience before they become second nature to the leader.

2. Begin with Baby Steps

"A journey of a thousand miles begins with a single step" is a common proverb. In this vein, those closest in the command heirarchy can start by taking small steps. Identify what decisions you can take independently and start from there. Eventually, you improve your decision-making muscle and build confidence for when you must step in the leader's shoes.

3. Take Charge When the Time Comes

Finally, when the boss is not around, do not allow a vacuum to develop. Work must carry on as usual, and take steps to ensure everything proceeds as per usual. This is the mark of a good deputy and a good leader—they understand the importance of mitigating overreliance on them.

This quote from a successful CEO sums it up best: "The master is gone, but he left behind masterpieces!"

WHEN TO SURRENDER

"A weak king, over-run by a strong king who has set his
armies in motion, should quickly submit, seeking peace
with [the offer of] his treasury, army, himself or territory."
(7.3.22)

We come back here to discuss strategies for war. Remember,
it is not just important to be strong, but also to be smart.
Look at the situation and also the context before deciding how to
deal with the enemy. In this sutra, we are considering a situation
where a weak king is dealing with a stronger king who has already
launched an offensive.

Later, when the right opportunity comes, the weak king
should attack the strong king and emerge a winner.

Let us see the explanation:

1. Know Your Limits

While valour is also given importance in Chanakya's philosophy,
knowing your limits and respecting the opponent's advantage is
the practical choice for any leader. They aren't merely fighting
for themselves but for those who depend on them. In light of this,

going in guns blazing may not always be the best tactic. Consider the situation to its last detail and decide the best course of action instead. You will find that, sometimes, you may have to respect the enemy's immense advantage and surrender control to avoid collateral damage.

2. Offer Appeasement to De-escalate

Find a way to de-escalate. Resorting to *dana*, allow the enemy to relent. Offer a peace treaty by proposing a gift of wealth, part of the workforce, army, or territory. However, do not consider this a final defeat—you are only buying time. Still not convinced? Read on.

3. Find a Way to Recoup and Rebuild

One of the names of Lord Krishna is Ranchod, meaning one who ran away (*chod*) from the battlefield (*ran*). This was done by Krishna not because he was afraid of the enemy but because he did not want his people to be killed, women to be dishonoured, and children to suffer. He was the king of Dwaraka, cared more for his people than his pride and, knew the value of taking a step back.

Likewise, it is better to keep options open for yourself than give in to the moment's heat. You will not be able to rebuild from a loss if you destroy yourself beforehand. If Krishna can do this, what's stopping you?

LIFELONG LESSONS

IMPORTANCE OF KNOWLEDGE FOR A LEADER

"Just as an elephant, blinded by intoxication and mounted by an intoxicated driver, crushes whatever it finds [on the way], so the king, not possessed of the eye of science, and [hence] blind, has risen to destroy the citizens and the country people." (1.14.7)

Chanakya uses elephants in this analogy to drive home a powerful point. He says that a bad leader in a powerful position is akin to an intoxicated mahout riding an intoxicated elephant. The elephant's sheer power, if not controlled, leads to chaos. Therefore, in the process, the elephant, the rider, and several others will be mowed down and destroyed. So, it is crucial that the leader resorts to reason and acts on knowledge.

Let us explore this further.

1. Gather Information and Analyse It

Information-gathering systems are critical for leaders to ensure they remain grounded and don't get drunk on power. Any information should get to them at the speed of thought.

However, do not stop there. Ensure that you understand the information received. Whether it is employee reports or expert opinion on an undertaking, the leader must scrutinise the information and choose what to act on, what to file away for later, and what to discard altogether.

2. Experiment

Whatever you learn, ensure that you apply it in the organisation. You could try a new method of executing a process, implement a new technology stack, and generally keep the stone rolling. As time passes, you will end up refining your organisation's systems with these tiny steps, making them more robust. In business parlance, this is called the "iterative process."

3. Ensure Information Trickles Down

One of the primary checks for power is keeping others who are just as knowledgeable and strong-minded around the leader. Learn to delegate important tasks from time to time and share your widening knowledge base with those that work with you. Doing so will ensure a two-way flow of ideas and feedback on any action, ensuring that the drunk mahout-and-elephant situation does not play out in the organisation.

THE ART OF CONTINUOUSLY EDUCATING OURSELVES

"During the remaining parts of the day and the night, he should learn new things and familiarise himself with those already learnt, and listen repeatedly to things not learnt." (1.5.15)

We all must remember the two roles of Chanakya. First, when he was a student at Takshashila University and topped the class. Then, as Chanakya, the great teacher. In both these roles, he retained a trait that made him the kingmaker of ancient India: being a perpetual learner.

Likewise, for modern leaders, the adage rings true: "What you do in your spare time determines your future." The hours at school, college, at work, or for other obligations take up a large chunk of your day. However, whether you focus on mindless leisure or engage in pursuit of growth will determine how your future pans out.

But how can you go down this path?

1. Join a Class or Take Up a Course

Take up professional weekend courses or opt for distance learning programs to further your knowledge of the field. This is especially important in modern times as many of us work in knowledge jobs where things change drastically every few years. Those who go down this route will ensure they aren't left behind in the marathon.

2. Read Books

MRI scans have confirmed that reading fires up a complex network of circuits in the brain. As you read more, these networks establish stronger connections and become more sophisticated. Likewise, reading helps you build empathy, an important resource in the diverse workplaces we are all a part of today. Other studies even confirm that just 30 minutes of reading a day reduces stress, lowering heart rate, blood pressure, and feelings of overall distress. Moreover, books can be among the most cost-effective ways to learn a new skill or pick up a new hobby.

3. Meet and Mingle with the Right People

As much importance as he places on learning, practical experience's immense importance is not lost on Chanakya. In other sutras, he has emphasised how critical company can be in a leader's growth. Being surrounded by yes men at all times will only solidify your negative traits. On the other hand, a leader who regularly consults experts and keeps one foot on the ground grows manifold and benefits those depending on them.

KEEP LEARNING AND APPLYING

"Continuous study ensures a trained intellect. From intellect [comes] practical application, [and] from practical application [results] self- possession." (1.5.16)

Next, Chanakya covers the benefits of engaging in perpetual learning. Here, he advises on the three benefits of perpetual learning: having a trained intellect, having the capability for practical application, and, finally, being self-possessed, or calm in the face of adversity.

Let us understand them briefly.

1. A Trained Intellect

As we have already established, the perpetual learner becomes incredibly knowledgeable owing to the small chunks of information they imbibe consistently over a long period. In a knowledge economy, this is akin to arming oneself.

2. Capable of Practical Application

Being good in theory is a good starting point but not enough. Your base and foundations become solid, but the proof is in the pudding, not the recipe. Chanakya considers this a natural next step in the learner's journey, as field experience often adds a whole new paradigm to the learnt theory.

A great master once said, "Knowing is not doing—doing is doing." Yes, do it yourself, and you will see the actual outcome. Once you experience the success of your practical application, you have a deeper understanding of the subject and become an expert.

3. Self-Possession

Have you heard of the Dunning-Kruger Effect? It states that people with low ability or expertise in a field tend to overestimate their abilties. As a result, they may end up fierce but misguided proponents of certain ideas. On the flip side, those with vast experience in a field often underestimate their ability and exercise greater humility in their dealings. Chanakya considers this humility and composure the final, definitive sign of a perpetual learner.

SETTING UP SYSTEMS IN YOUR NEW JOB

"He should institute a righteous custom, not initiated before and continue one initiated by others, and he should not institute an unrighteous custom, and should stop any initiated by others." (13.5.24)

What is the duty of a leader? To continue what the previous leaders have started, and also to create something new by themselves. In this sutra, Chanakya reveals the foolproof method of ensuring you leave a legacy behind. This is how you become a great leader.

Let us see how to follow this as a leader.

1. Which Practices to Continue

The itch to make sweeping changes is palpable when a new leader assumes power. However, they must possess the critical eye that understands which practices of the predecessor were actually good, regardless of individual differences. Such objectivity will also ensure you do not shake things up too much and alienate employees who have been around for a long time.

2. Which Practices to Denounce

Every country has certain cultures and traditions. These may be righteous or unrighteous. Chanakya directs budding leaders to weed out the unrighteous, outdated customs. For instance, marriages are part of our social fabric in India. However, child marriages are unrighteous, and social leaders worked hard and eradicate the custom.

Likewise, in an organisation, you are bound to find policies that do not align with the right values. If in a position of power, you must work to weed them out.

Chanakya also extends this advice and warns against instituting such unjust practices yourself, lest they taint your legacy and render your hard work meaningless.

3. Which Practices to Institute

Institute new practices that address existing problems and improve the bottom line or the workers' lives. In this manner, the leader will grow to be loved and strengthen the company. A classic example of such leadership is seen in the Tata Group. After taking the torch from J. R. D. Tata, Ratan Tata instituted new practices that grew the company manifold.

These questions may also lead to ethical dilemmas, also called *dharma sankat*. In Chanakya's opinion, the preferred way of resolving this should be after discussions with elders, experts, or mentors.

THE WAY TO IMPROVE WHAT YOU INHERIT

"In the case of inherited territory, he should cover up the father's defects and display his virtues." (13.5.23)

Fortunate are those who inherit property and other assets from their ancestors and forefathers who were "first-generation entrepreneurs." Though these fledgling businessmen may not have to struggle much in life, they must understand what they are inheriting and capitalise on it to further the previous generation's vision.

Here's the advice he offers.

1. Identify the Positive Aspects

The first-generation entrepreneur has likely already done the most difficult work—building from scratch by doing market research, finding a product that fits, obtaining licenses and setting up facilities, capturing the market, and so on. As we all know now, these stages are rife with difficult situations. There may have been times when a now-flourishing company once had a shoestring budget.

More than the orgnisation itself, this history is the greatest inheritance. It shines light on the mistakes of the previous generation and informs you on *what not to do*. In identifying this and acting to avoid these errors, the heir already has a significant headstart over their predecessors.

2. Negate the Negatives

What if you inherit something that is ill-reputed or has a bad name? There is no point blaming the previous generation now. Understand where they went wrong and go easy—after all, they lived in very different times than yours. The culture, government policies, and market conditions were all different then.

Suppose you inherit a business that was once illegitimate. Maybe it was not considered illegitimate or illegal in the previous generation and in that socio-economic scenario. You have a responsibility here: to bring goodwill to your family by making a turnaround to doing only legitimate business.

Focus on what next. What you do with it is your creativity and productivity.

3. Be the Source of Positive Change

You should also know how to *create* a good reputation. Following your own set of values and ethics, start elevating the organisation to newer heights. Maintain relations within the business with clients and employees, both old and new, ensuring that you become a role model for them in the process.

Learn to give back to society as well. Doing so will not only generate goodwill but improve society in incremental steps, thus helping your business in the long term.

There was once a businessman who came from a humble background. After many years of struggle, fortune blessed him with wealth, and he became very rich. He went to his father sharing the good news the day it happened. His father did not seem impressed and enquired, "If you have become rich, my question is—are you ready to share your wealth with the less privileged?" Though this was a tough pill to swallow, the businessman began giving to charity and, surprisingly, his wealth only grew. This simple tale reiterates the principle of being rich forever: "The more you give, the more you get back."

KEEP AN OPEN MIND TO GET GREAT IDEAS

"He should despise none, [but] should listen to the opinion of every one. A wise man should make use of the sensible words of even a child." (1.15.22)

Finally, we come to the final sutra we have selected from the 6,000 in the Arthashastra. This offers us the basis for imbibing Chanakya's teachings in our lives: be open-minded. If you want to be intelligent like Chanakya, you need to identify and respect the intellect of others as well.

After all, one never knows when or where the next big idea will come from. Therefore, effective listening is critical for any leader.

Let us look at this final sutra in detail:

1. He Should Despise None

Never look down on anyone. Respect all and approach conversations without preconceived notions about the other party. Many leaders use this approach to gather information at the top and grassroots levels. They have the ability to meet with business tycoons one moment and hear the complaints of an entry-level employee the next. It is difficult to practise this in the beginning, but with effort and patience, it will become your nature. From a spiritual standpoint, consider everyone as a creation of God.

2. Respond, Don't React

Even if you hear something that contradicts your opinion or levels criticism, learn not to react. Many people fall for this trap by entering a conversation with the will to *reply*, sacrificing their ability to actually understand what the other person is saying. This is a destructive trait. Not only is cutting someone off mid-conversation disrespectful, but it could also cause the conversation to end abruptly, and you may have missed valuable information that was coming your way. Therefore, listen fully and intently to what the other person says. To reinforce this idea, Chanakya suggests that one must consider a child's opinion.

3. Make Use of the Ideas You Learn

The best ideas will fail if they remain mere thoughts. Likewise, information is useless unless you can scrutinise it and see how it may be used to your benefit. An extension of this is to not be afraid of experimentation: unless the rubber meets the asphalt, how would you know the idea can hold its own in the market? So use the wisdom Chanakya imparts to you and take calculated risks instead. That is how you succeed, the Chanakya way.

ABOUT THE AUTHOR

RADHAKRISHNAN PILLAI is the bestselling author of *Corporate Chanakya, Chanakya's 7 Secrets of Leadership, Chanakya in You, Katha Chanakya, Thus Spoke Chanakya,* and *Chanakya Neeti.* He has a master's degree in Sanskrit and has completed his Ph.D in Kautilya's Arthashastra. A renowned management consultant and speaker, he is the founder and director of the Chanakya International Institute of Leadership Studies (CIILS) at the University of Mumbai, as well as the chief mentor of his leadership training and consulting firm, Chanakya Aanvikshiki Pvt. Ltd.

He tweets using the handle @rchanakyapillai and is also active on other major social media platforms.

JAICO PUBLISHING HOUSE

Elevate Your Life. Transform Your World.

ESTABLISHED IN 1946, Jaico Publishing House is home to world-transforming authors such as Sri Sri Paramahansa Yogananda, Osho, the Dalai Lama, Sri Sri Ravi Shankar, Sadhguru, Robin Sharma, Deepak Chopra, Jack Canfield, Eknath Easwaran, Devdutt Pattanaik, Khushwant Singh, John Maxwell, Brian Tracy, and Stephen Hawking.

Our late founder Mr. Jaman Shah first established Jaico as a book distribution company. Sensing that independence was around the corner, he aptly named his company Jaico ('Jai' means victory in Hindi). In order to service the significant demand for affordable books in a developing nation, Mr. Shah initiated Jaico's own publications. Jaico was India's first publisher of paperback books in the English language.

While self-help, religion and philosophy, mind/body/spirit, and business titles form the cornerstone of our non-fiction list, we publish an exciting range of travel, current affairs, biography, and popular science books as well. Our renewed focus on popular fiction is evident in our new titles by a host of fresh young talent from India and abroad. Jaico's recently established translations division translates selected English content into nine regional languages.

Jaico distributes its own titles. With its headquarters in Mumbai, Jaico has branches in Ahmedabad, Bangalore, Chennai, Delhi, Hyderabad, and Kolkata.

SINCE 1946